AN ANTHOLOGY OF ASEMIC HANDWRITING.

printed by lightning source, milton keynes
in an endless edition (version ~~130826~~, 140209)
ISBN 978-90-817091-7-0

uitgeverij, den haag
shtëpia botuese, tiranë
publishing house, adelaide & minneapolis

www.uitgeverij.cc

An Anthology of Asemic Handwriting.

EDITED BY TIM GAZE
AND MICHAEL JACOBSON.

:

Preface

An Anthology of Asemic Handwriting presents a mixture of handwriting styles, from many corners of the world, dating from the Chinese Tang Dynasty (618–907 CE) to the present day. The tendency toward illegibility exists in many cultural traditions, and in this anthology we intend to offer a representative overview of the different styles, and, more specifically, the contemporary developments in asemic handwriting. We deliberately avoided the adjectives "unreadable" and "illegible" in the title of this anthology, because the question of legibility and possible transference of meaning is precisely what is at stake in these writing traditions. These writings are not completely "meaningless" or "illegible," but challenge our common notions of reading, writing, and the meaningfulness of language. Therefore we prefer the adjective "asemic." In the late 20th century, this word was handed down from the poet John Byrum to another poet named Jim Leftwich to one of the editors of this anthology.

Western people are often unfamiliar with the fact that the term calligraphy, which literally means "beautiful writing," can also be applied to wild, noisy examples of handwriting. For example, the famous Chinese calligrapher "Crazy" Zhāng Xù, who enjoyed copious amounts of wine to loosen his spirit, wrote exuberant, energetic cursive calligraphy, in a style which became known as "crazy grass style." The morning after a writing session, Zhang often couldn't read his own writing. A younger man from the same era, "Mad Monk" Huái Sù, perfected his own style of illegible cursive. Whereas China is considered to be the matrix for calligraphy in Eastern Asia, separate strong traditions have arisen in other countries such as Japan, Korea, and Vietnam. Within these separate traditions, Zen Buddhism has been an influence away from legibility and toward power in brush writing.

Islamic calligraphy, whose origin is sometimes credited to the Bektashi dervishes, often distorts letters in fantastic ways toward being unreadable, even in the case of Qur'anic calligraphy. Ahmed Shibrain of Khartoum, known for his abstract renditions of Qur'anic suras, has a reputation as a graphic designer as well as an artist, whereas Rashid Koraishi, currently of Tunisia, includes Berber symbols and invented pictographs alongside his Arabic letters. The drive toward illegibility here is not so much influenced by the egoless flow of energy advocated in Zen Buddhism, but is rather informed by the extensive pictorial tradition within Islamic calligraphy, which itself is a result of the prohibition, in certain Islamic traditions, on depiction of human figures. Thus, even though different calligraphic traditions end up producing unreadable signs, the impetus toward illegibility varies widely.

Within Western handwriting traditions, asemic writing is – apart from a few singular exceptions, such as the Voynich manuscript – closely linked to a poetic practice that first liberated itself from the linearity of the verse, and subsequently from the conformity of the sign. Visual poetry, which plays with the forms of writing rather than concentrating solely on words, includes a healthy number of handwritten poems, of which a smaller proportion is asemic. A few names to mention from the 20th century are Christian Dotremont, Carlfriedrich Claus, and Robert Corydon.

Under the influence of mescaline (we again find here the relation between a drug-induced state and asemic writing), Henri Michaux worked extensively with his own symbols, as well as writing poetry and prose with his own strange vocabulary of words, drawing, painting with a brush, and splattering ink to create abstract paintings. This brings us to the second line of inquiry in the Western world which has led to illegible forms of writing, namely a tradition concerned with "mark making," and a broader analysis of the function of (spontaneous) gesture in modern art. Thus, visual artists from movements as far apart as Dada, Russian Futurism, Surrealism, CoBrA, Tachisme, Fluxus, Abstract Expressionism, Gutai, and Lettrisme have created asemic handwritten forms.

The origins of *An Anthology of Asemic Handwriting* can be traced back to the last two decades. Since 1998, Tim Gaze has published a magazine for asemic writing and related art forms, titled *Asemic*, which has grown from a folded four-page pamphlet to a hundred-page paperback book. Through its extensive distribution by mail, this magazine has sown the seeds for an international community of contemporary asemic writers.

Asemic magazine included the contact details (both physical mail and email) of nearly all of the contributors, forming an open source community or network. Mail artists, along with experimental poetry magazines such as *Generator* and *Selby's*

List were already using this free and open sharing of addresses as a means of speedily disseminating culture without editors or publishers acting as gatekeepers.

Asemic magazine's sister website www.asemic.net has been online since 2000, and although the content hasn't changed for years, it has acted as a piece of internet history, showing one stage of the evolution of the culture of asemic writing. The list of suggested search terms there, ranging from "abstract calligraphy" to "Zhang Xu Crazy Zhang wild cursive" (sic) continues to attract people with an interest in any of the artists or terms listed, before they know the word "asemic." Probably more than the magazine, the website has helped to amalgamate a much wider confluence from a number of previously separate streams of culture.

In 2008 Michael Jacobson, with the help of Tim Gaze and Derek Beaulieu, started an online gallery for asemic writing, under the flag of Marshall McLuhan's concept of the "post-literate." Asemic writing demands a consciousness of writing that entails a break with (traditional forms of) literacy, hence the title: *The New Post-Literate: A Gallery Of Asemic Writing*. This gallery has been online since, and has acted as a galvanizing place for the makers already associated with *Asemic*, as well as a new generation of artists, poets, and writers who use it as a common platform. Its frequent updates suggest a flourishing global community of asemic writers. Moreover, the word "asemic" itself seems to have some traction, being used increasingly in the English internet, and translations of it having been published in various literary journals, art magazines and opinion blogs, in languages such as French, Russian, Hungarian, Portuguese, Spanish, Italian, Dutch, Danish and Finnish.

With *An Anthology of Asemic Handwriting*, we are at the peak of the snowy mountain. It is an international mountain where there are no borders, fences, or walls. People have contributed to it from around the world, and across time. It is an anthology that belongs to a global network of writers, readers, artists, and explorers; of which there are over one hundred represented in this book.

This anthology only features a subset of the wide variety of asemic works, namely those forms which are made by leaving a mark on a surface applied by movements of the hand. We thus momentarily step away from machines, to highlight the myriad of forms of asemic writing currently happening outside the reach of modern technology. This is a step backward and a step forward at the same time. Other methods for achieving asemic writing, such as the analogue art of collage or various digital means of composition, will no doubt be featured in future publications.

Tim Gaze, Editor
Michael Jacobson, Editor
Vincent W.J. van Gerven Oei, Publisher

REED ALTEMUS

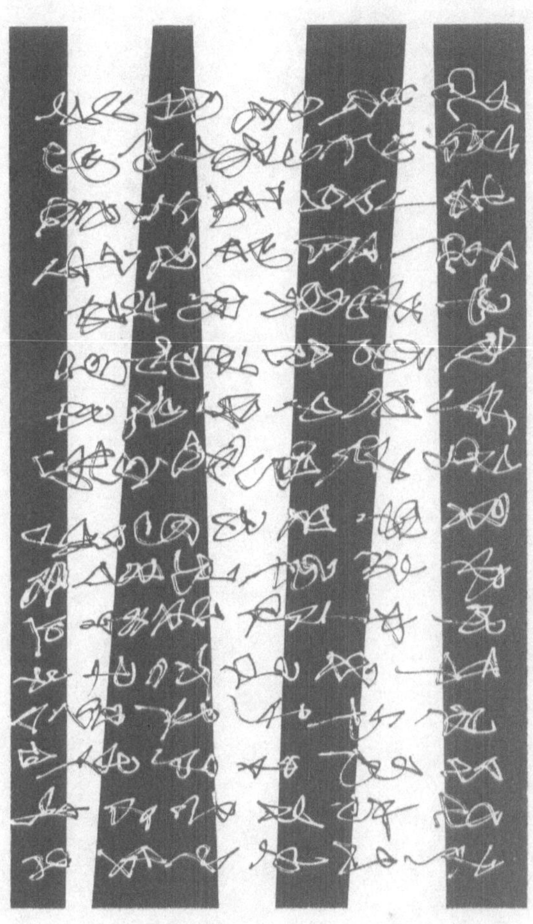

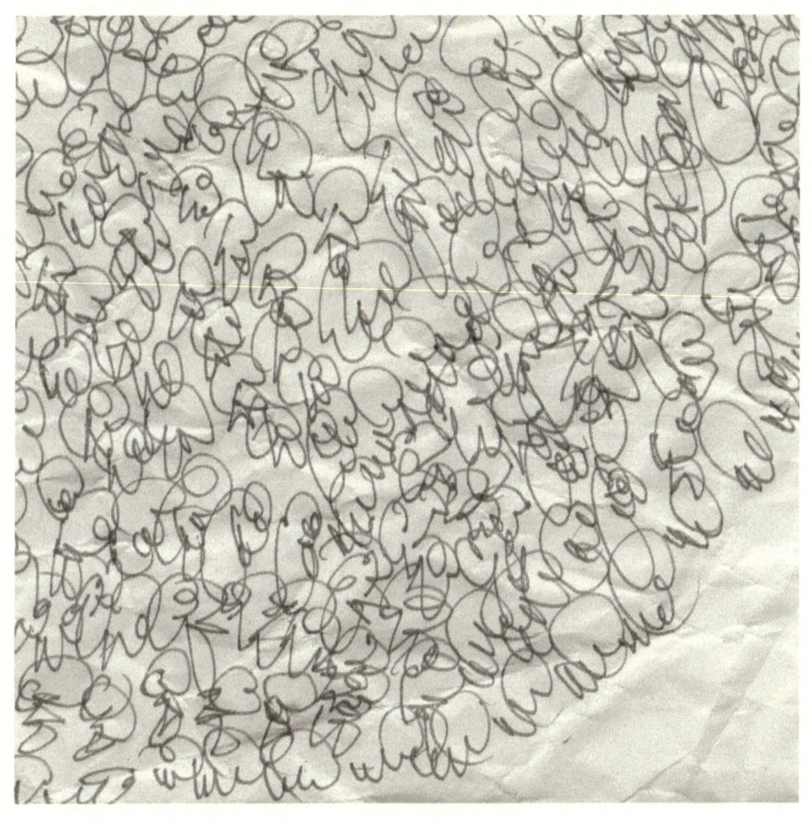

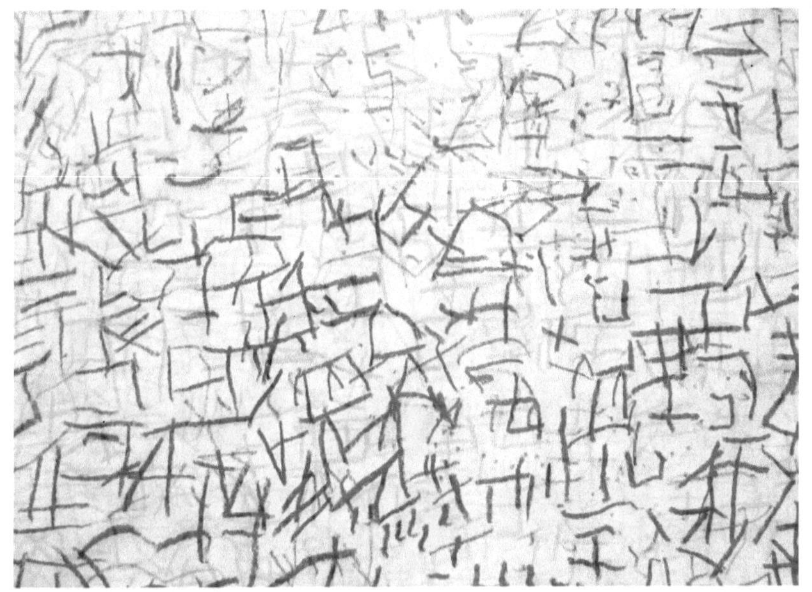

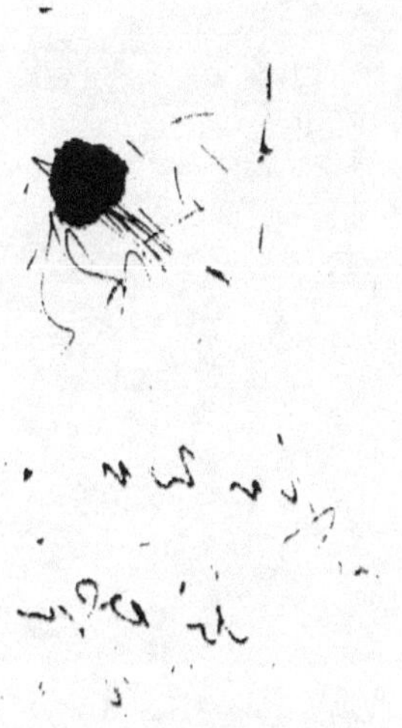

ROY ARENELLA

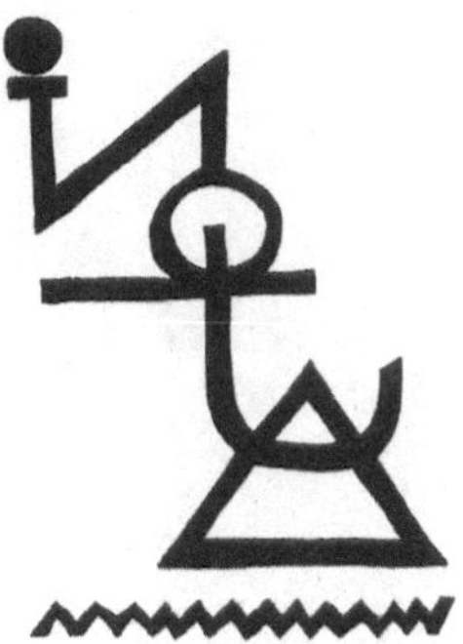

ROY ARENELLA

DEC. 8 2004

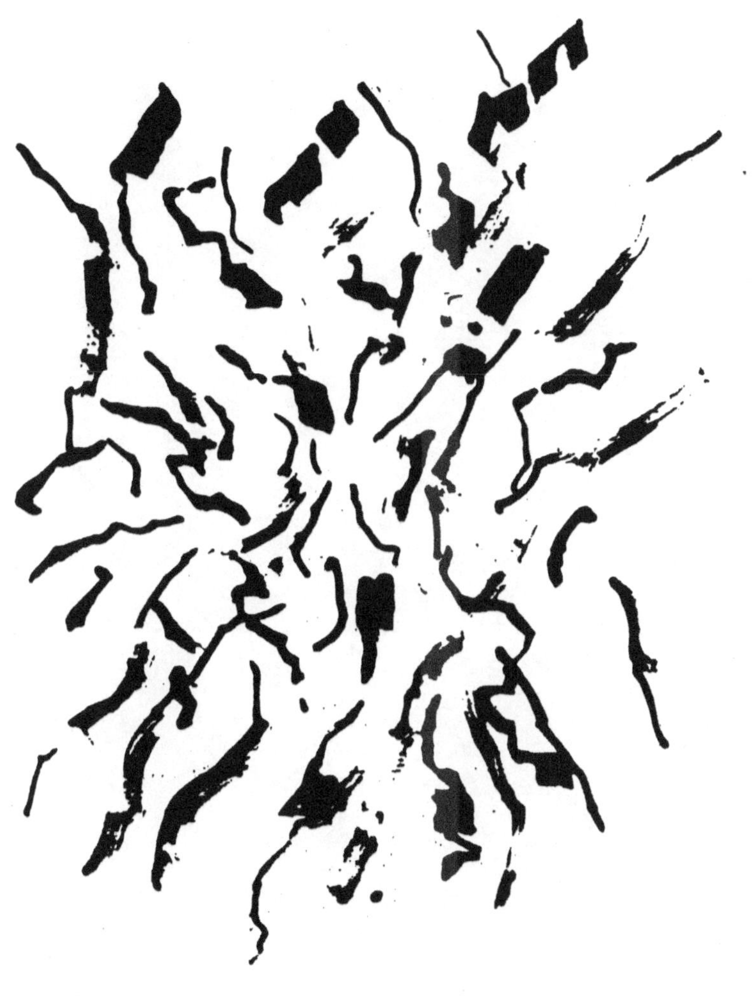

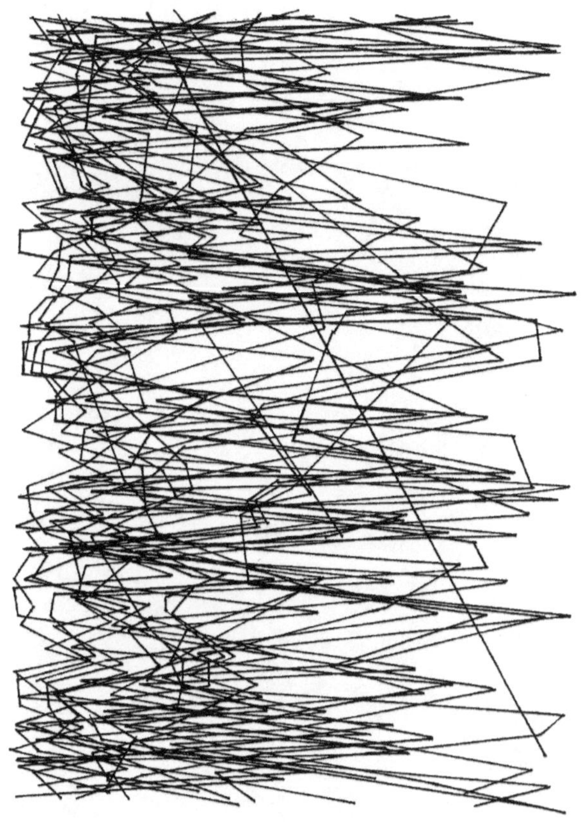

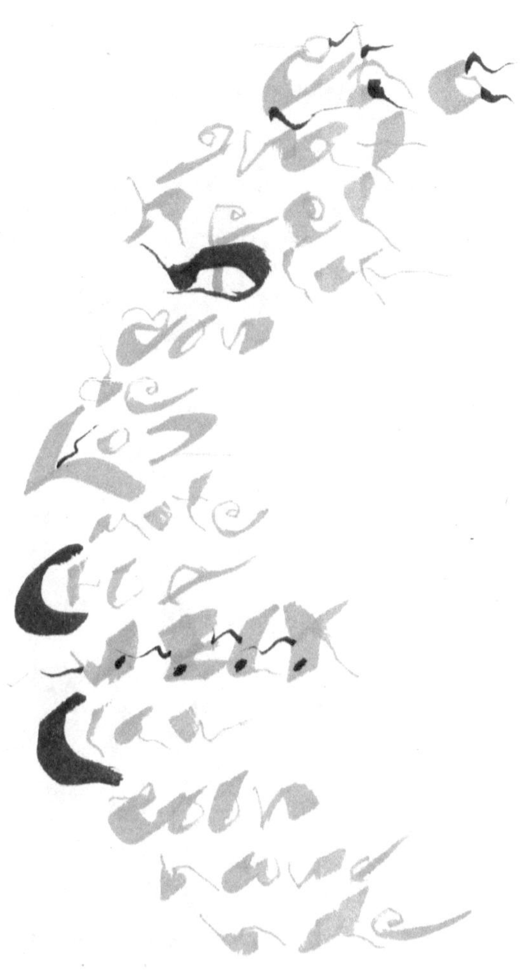

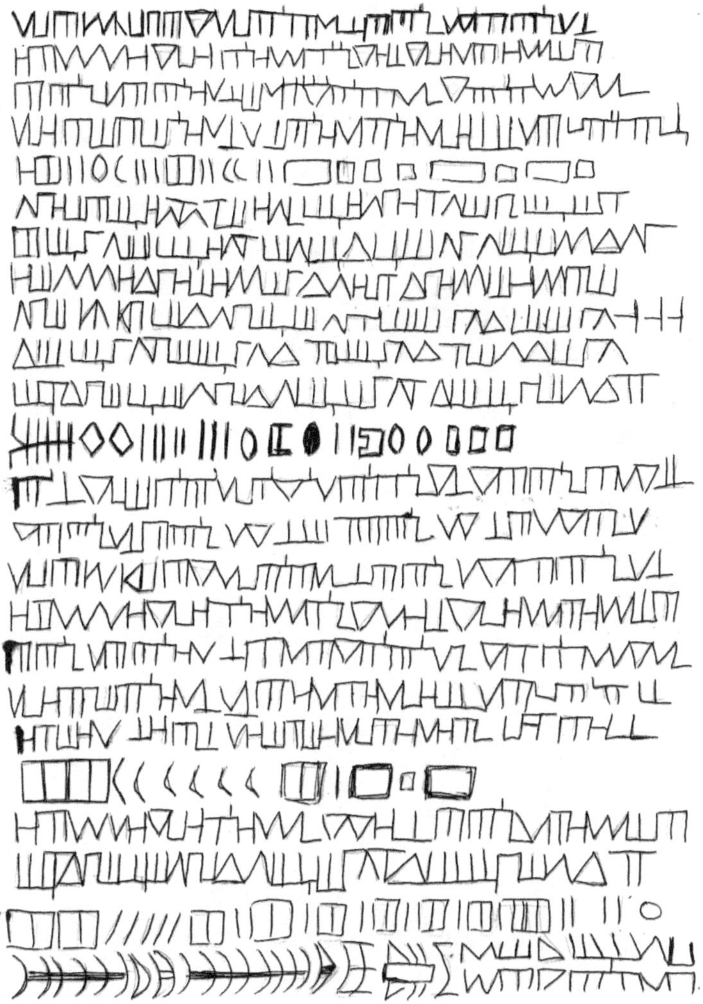

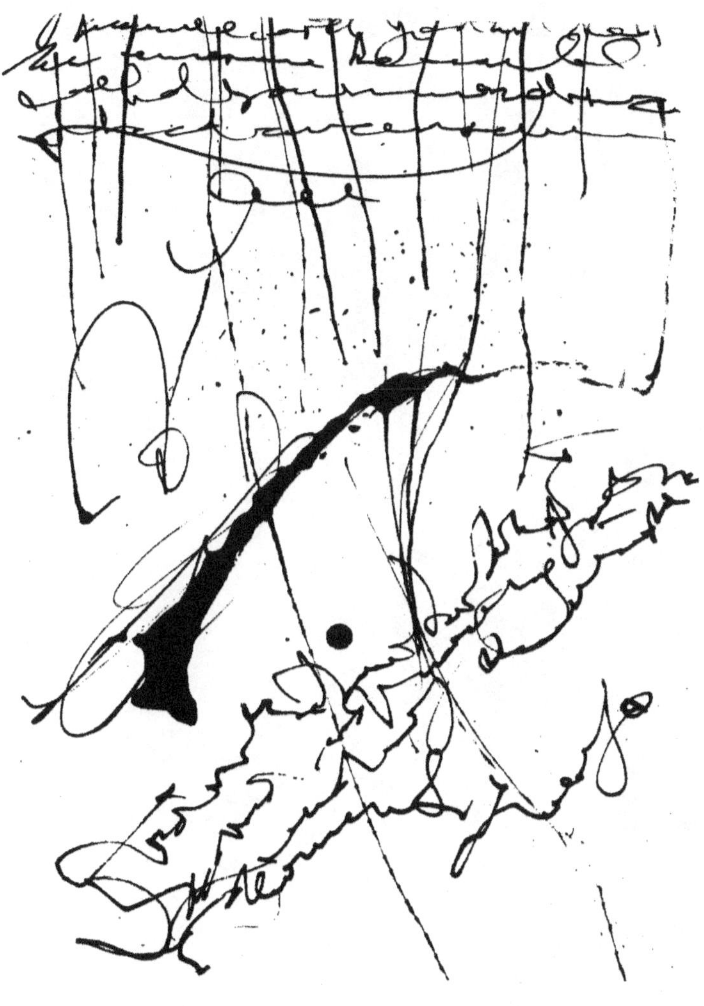

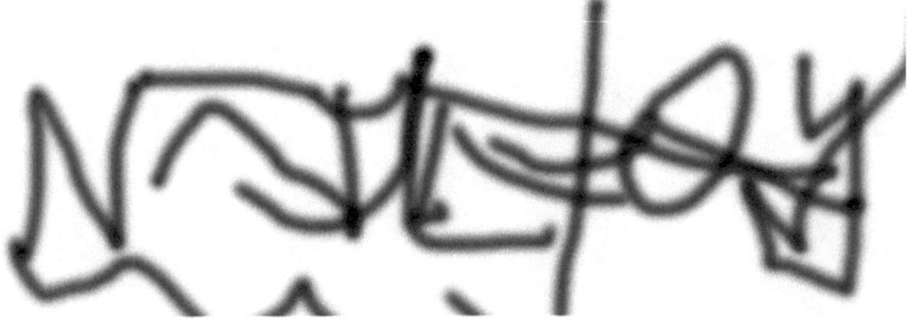

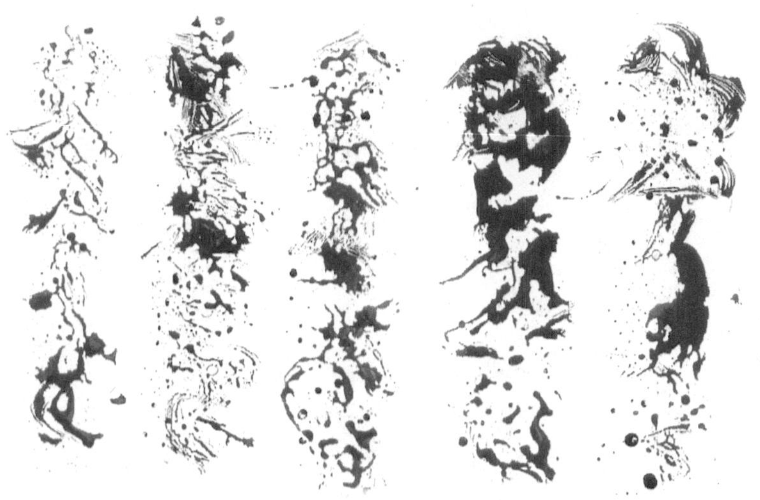

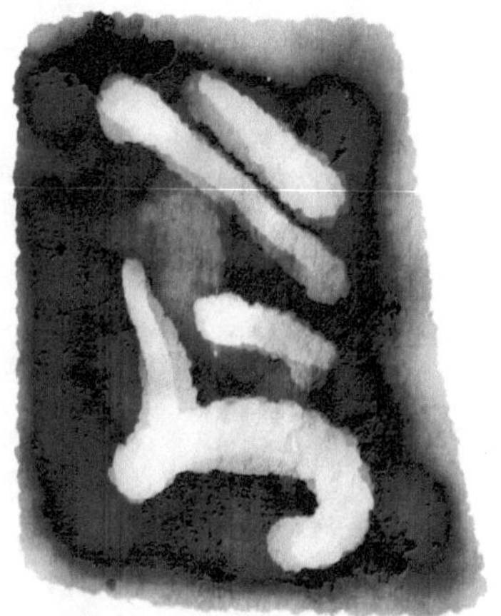

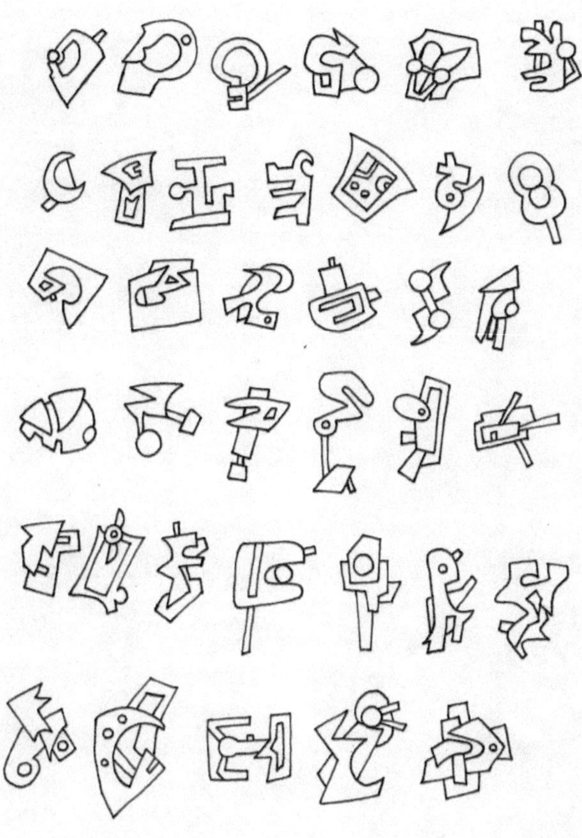

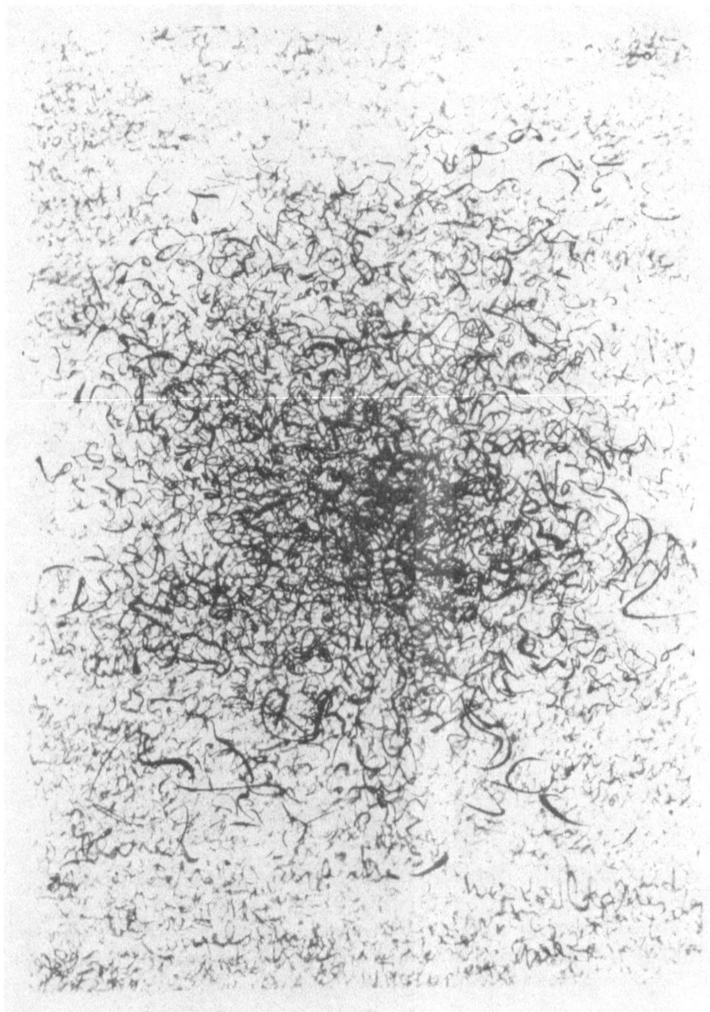

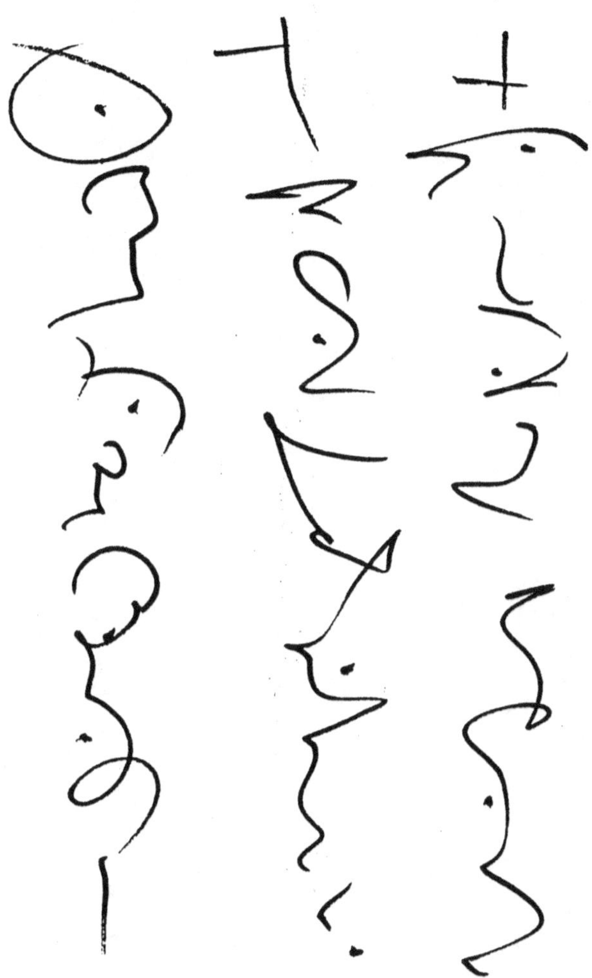

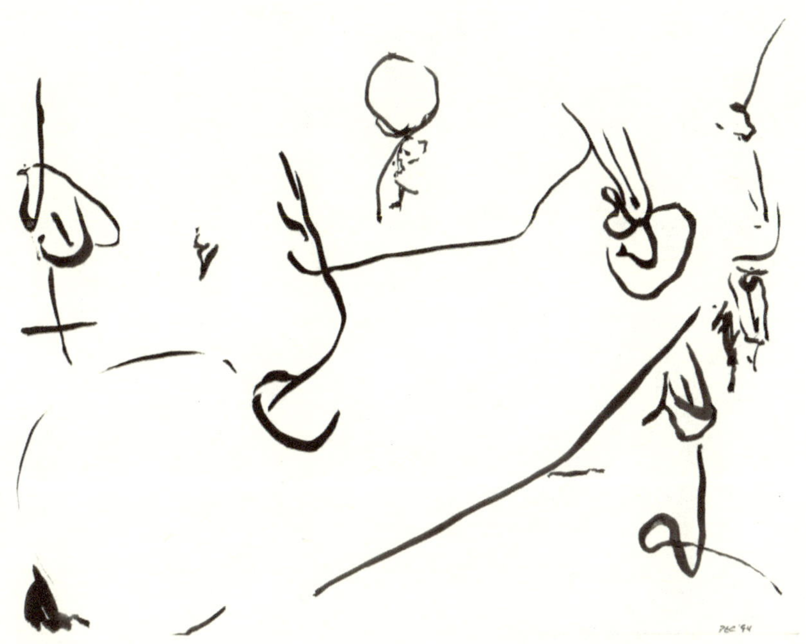

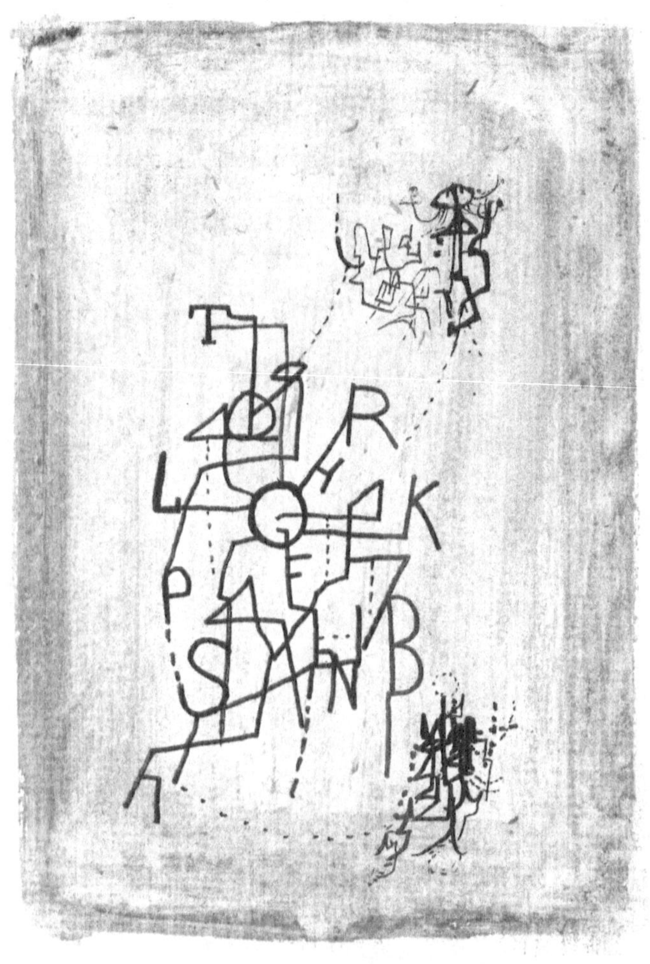

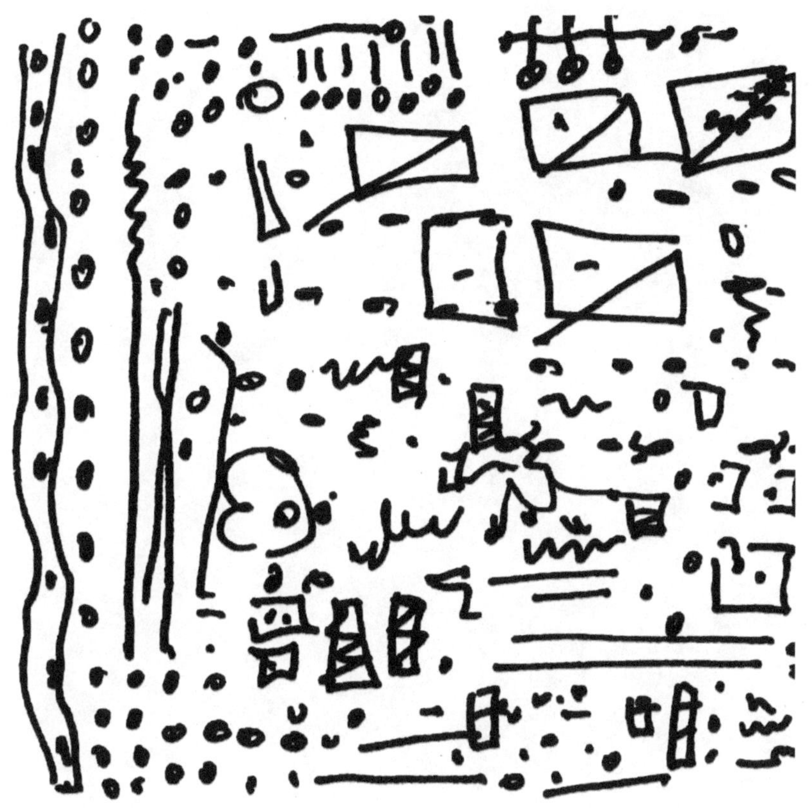

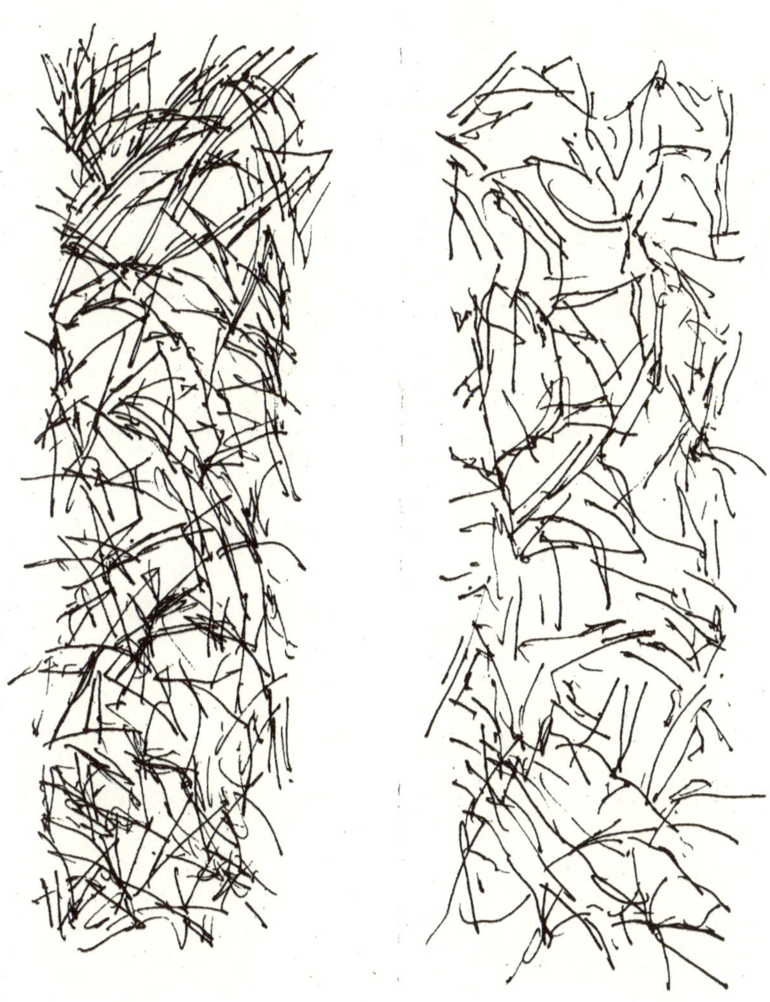

Lord everlasting, when he laid out the
who tried to compose sacred worlds.
but none of them could equal first raised ... the race
because his instruction ... heaven as roof, the ...
not ... all from men, nor through the world below, the ...
aid ... man, but ... mankind,
divine inspiration and ... Lord everlasting at last established
God that he received ... for man the Almighty Lord.
song. For that reason he was
able to compose poetry ... he arose from his sleep, and
idle nature, but only the one kind he had sung while asleep he
pertained to religion and was ... and soon after-
the ... godly ... words like unto
This man had lived ... to God. The
... he was some ... came to the steward
in years, and had ... his master and told him of
songs. For this reason ... he had received. The steward
... where ... led him to the abbess and
... that they should ... heard. She bade
sing in turn at the harp, when all the wise and learned men
would see the harp approach him Caedmon to relate his dream
would arise from the company presence and to sing the song
shame and ... his house ... judgment
one occasion he had done ... whence it had
left the banquet hall and gone ... was a
the stable to the cattle which ... bestowed from ... ven.
his duty ... that night. The ... explained to him a piece of
due time he lay down and slept, ... and bade him if he
then ... him in his dream ... turn that into rhythmic
man ... hailed him and greeted ... when he received the instruc-
and called him by name: "Caed

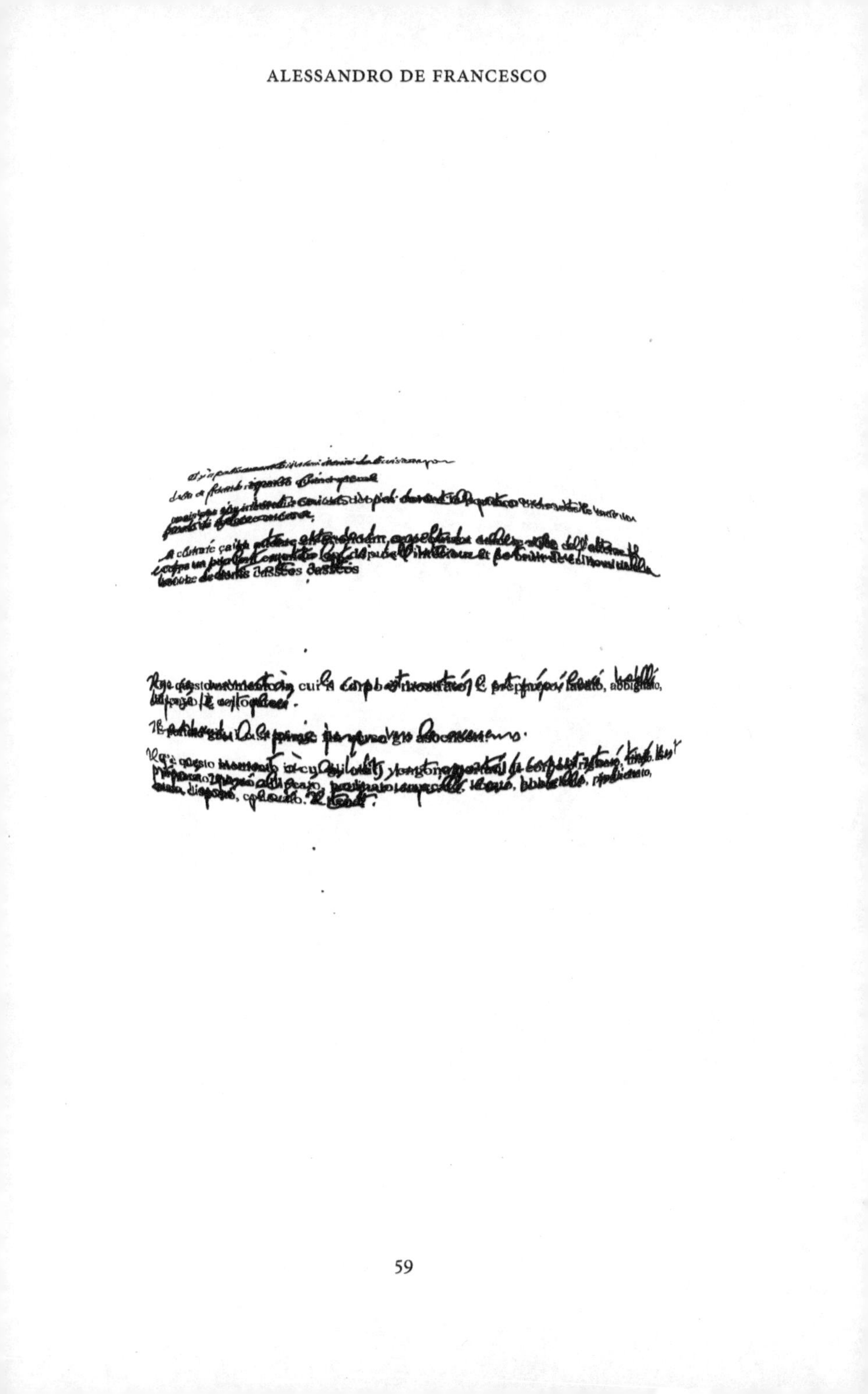

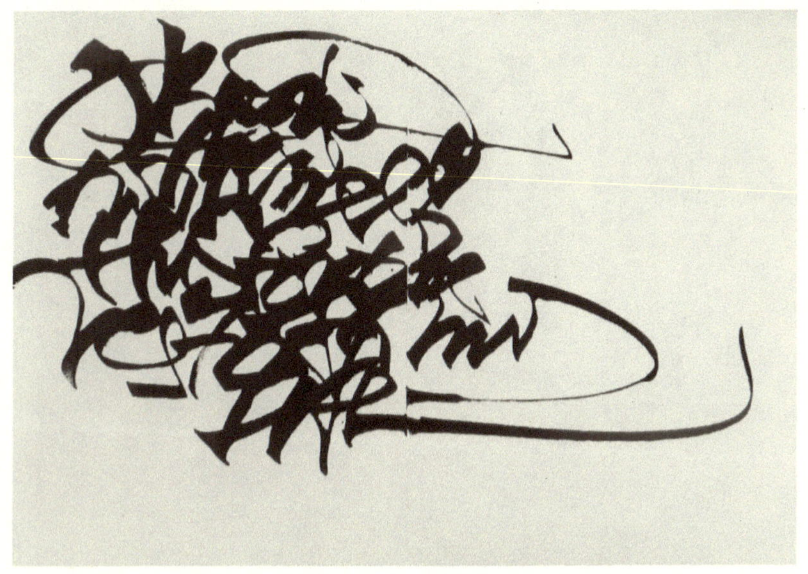

MIRTHA DERMISACHE

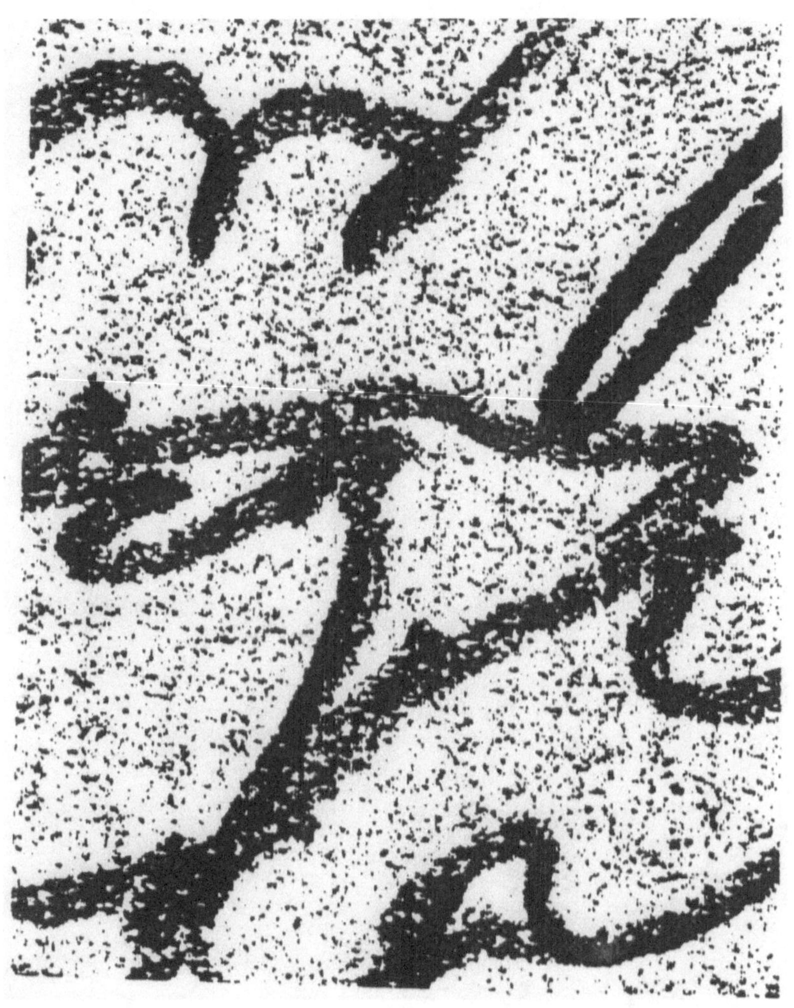

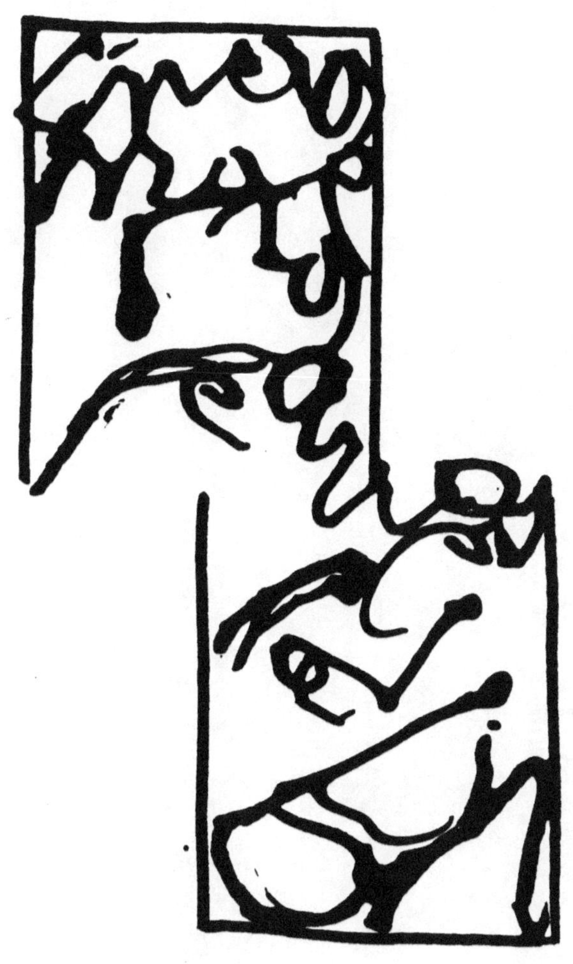

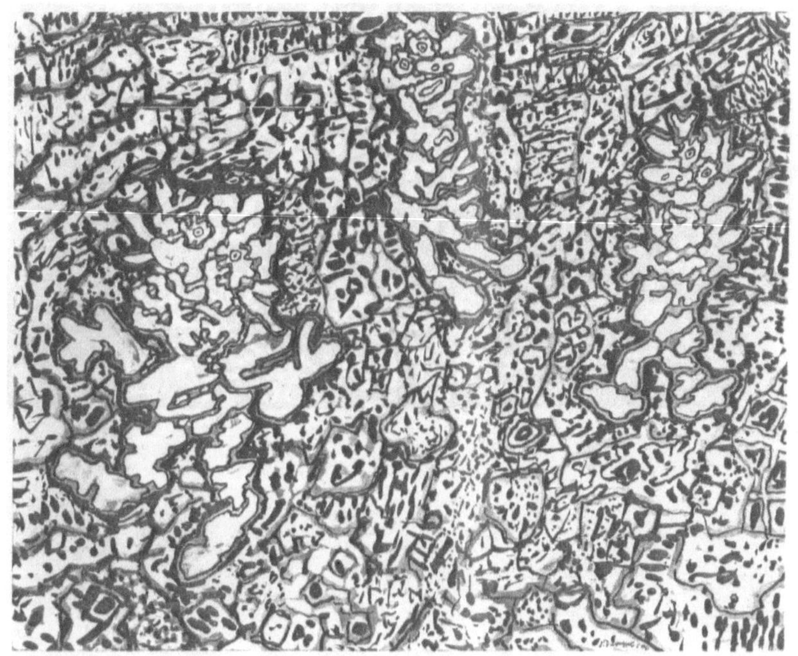

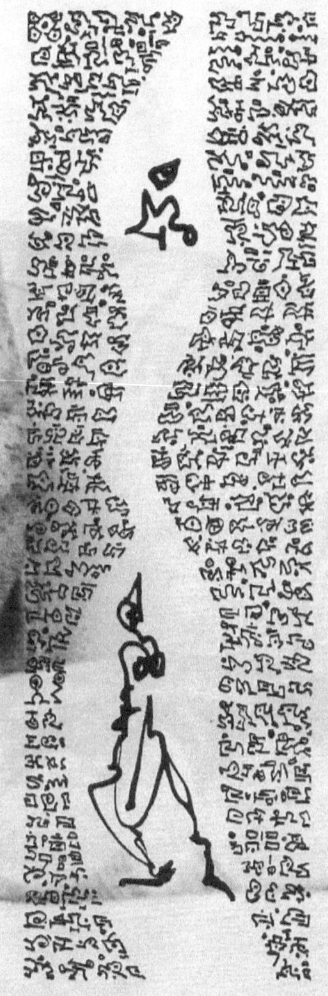

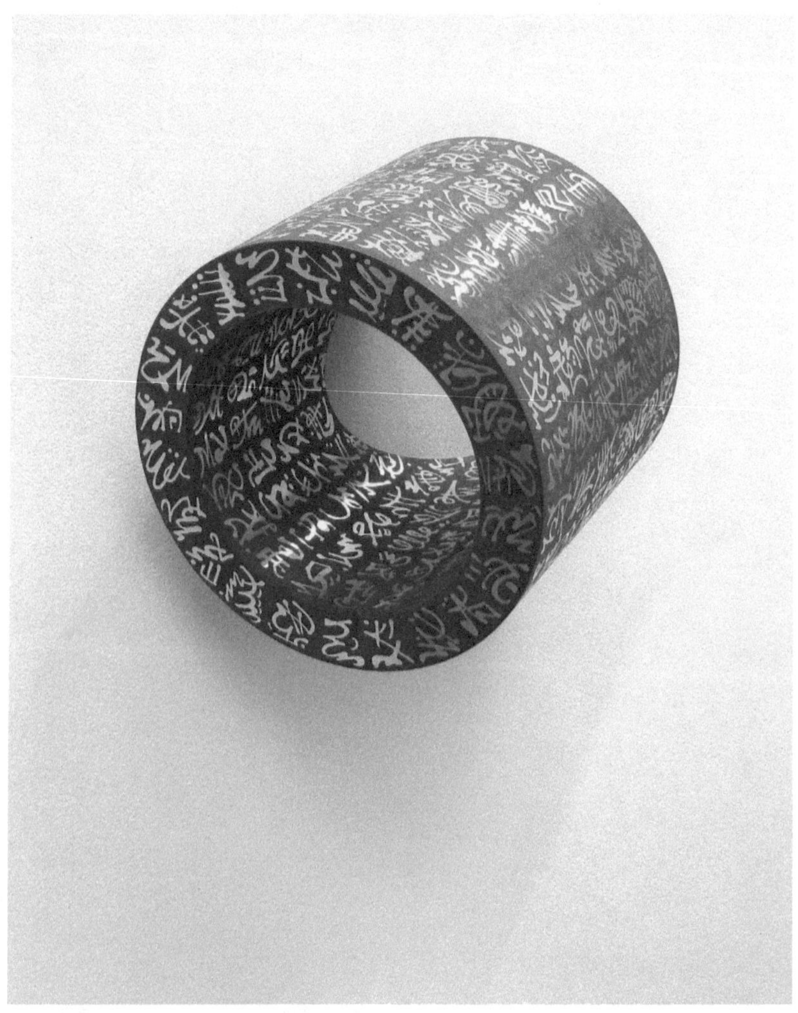

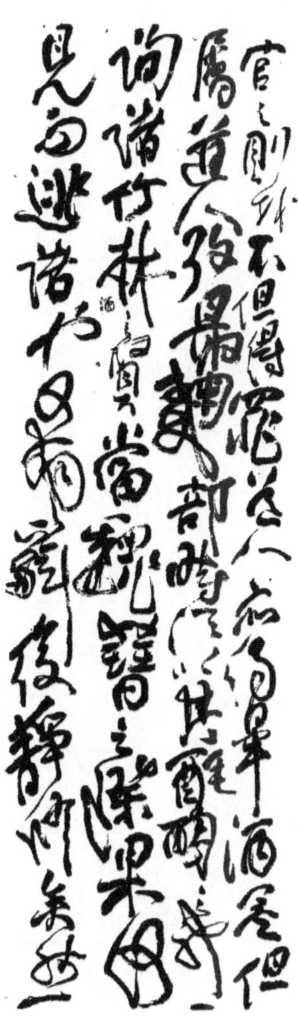

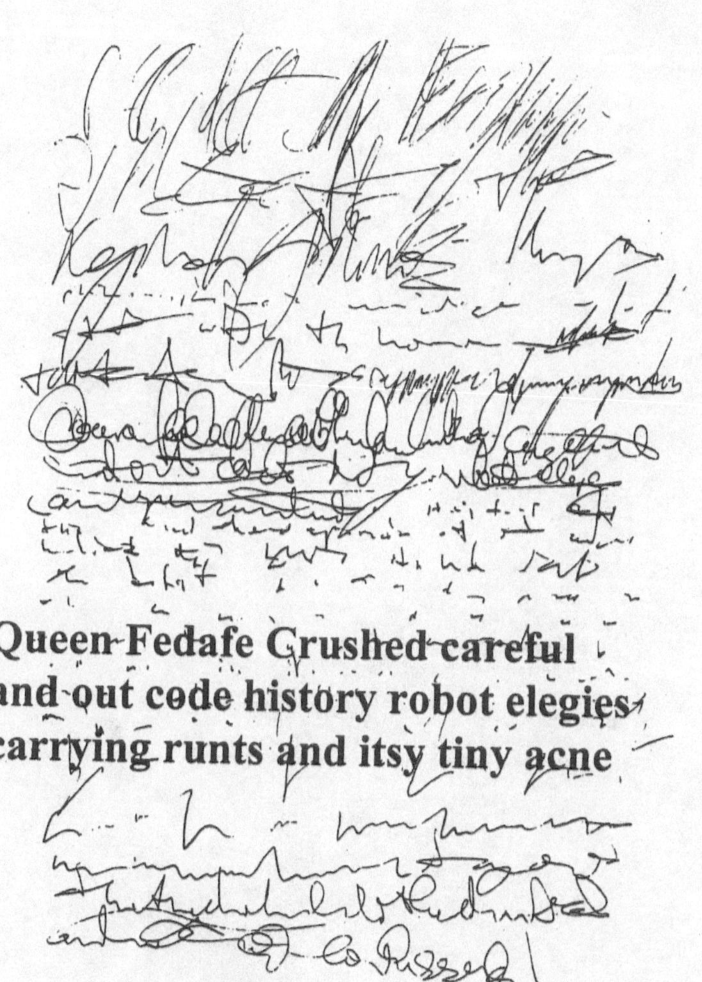
Queen Fedafe Crushed careful
and out code history robot elegies
carrying runts and itsy tiny acne

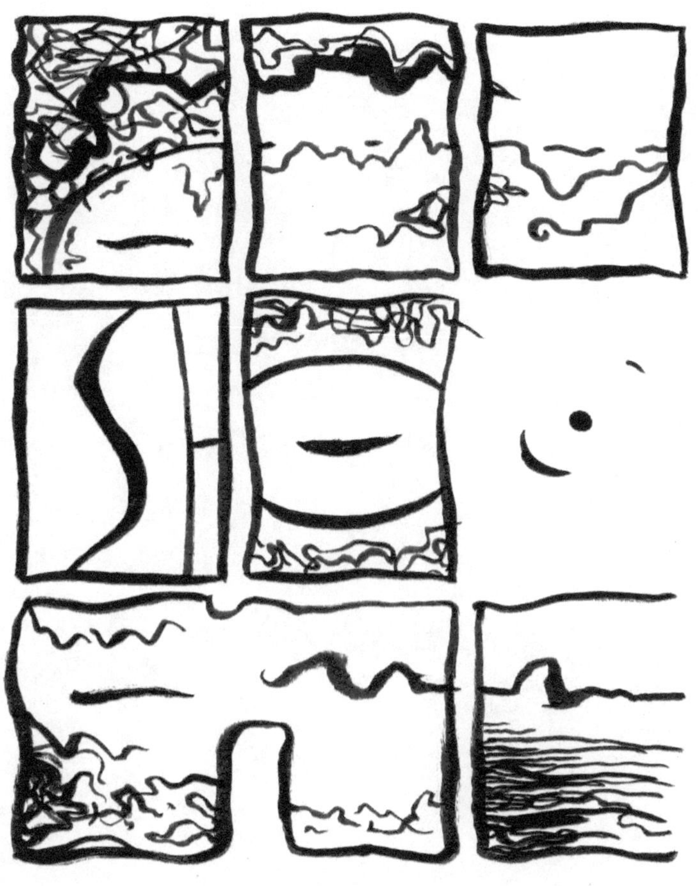

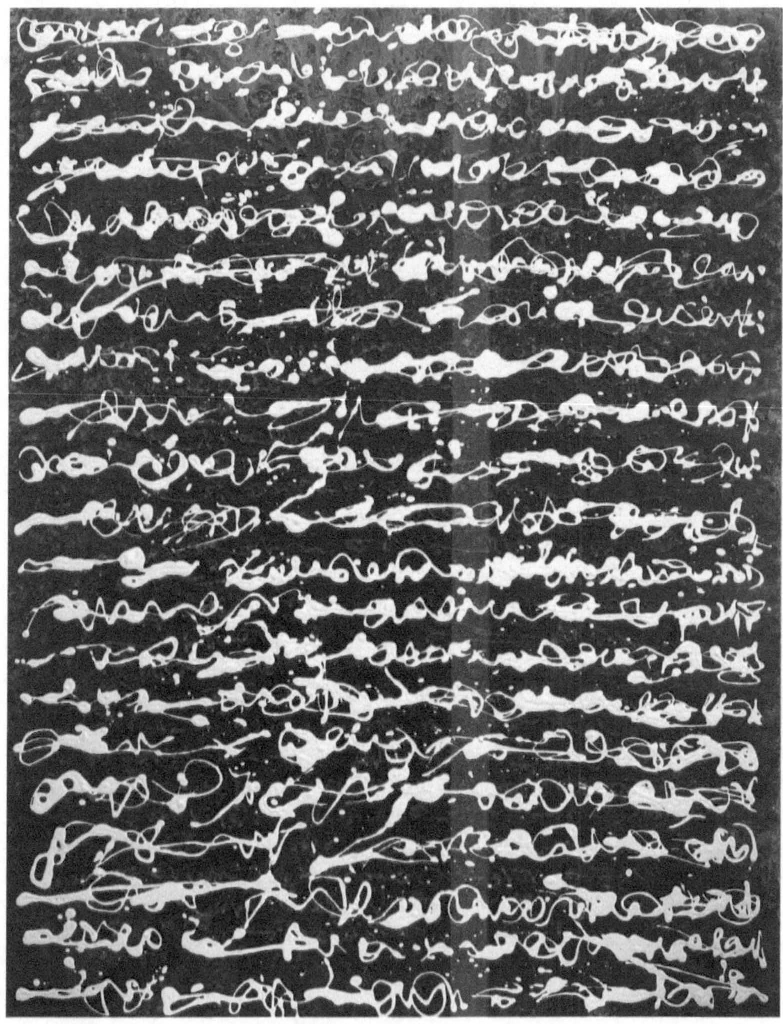

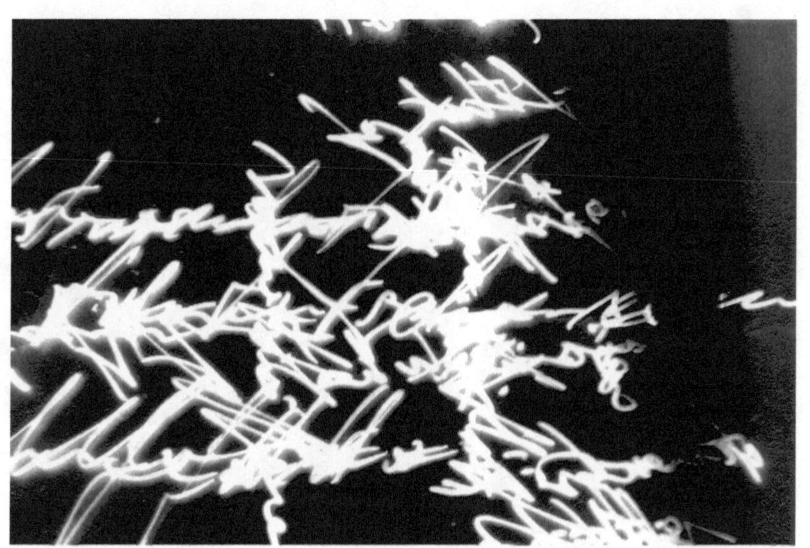

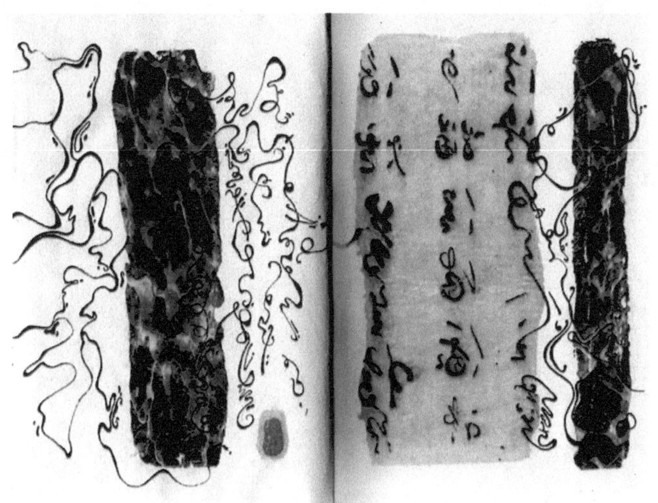

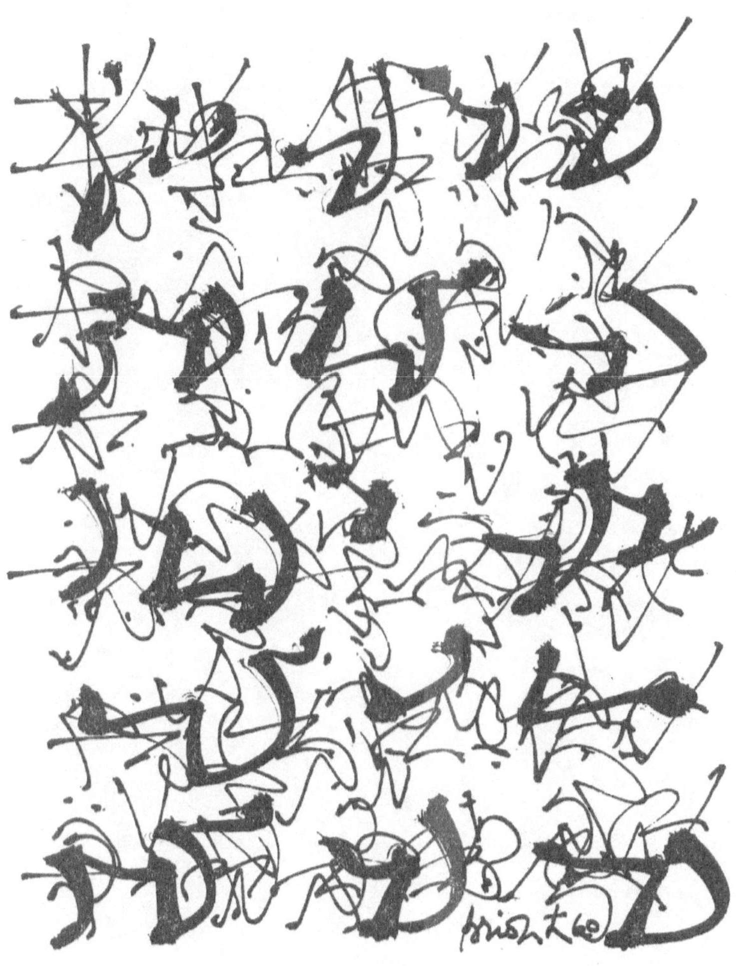

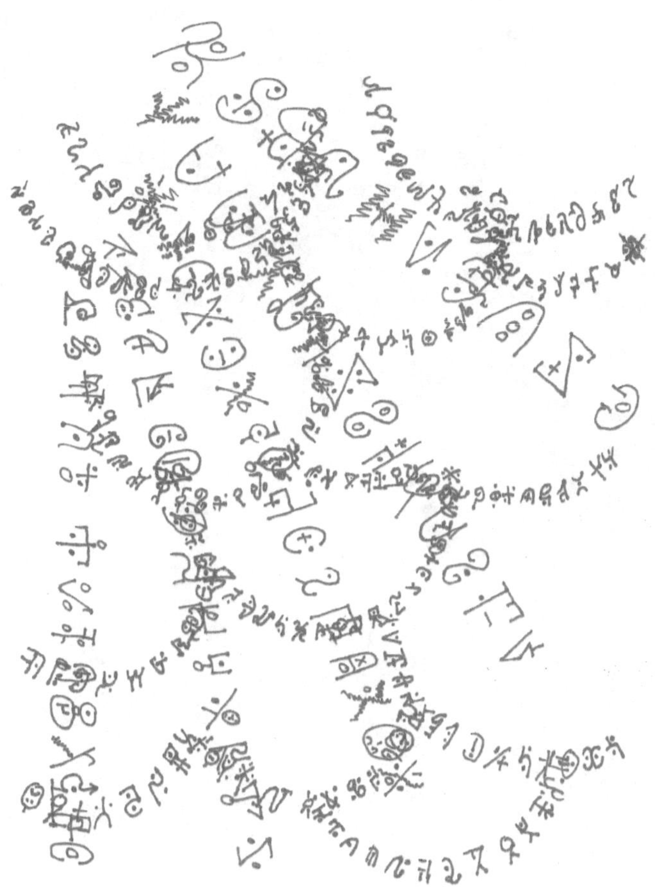

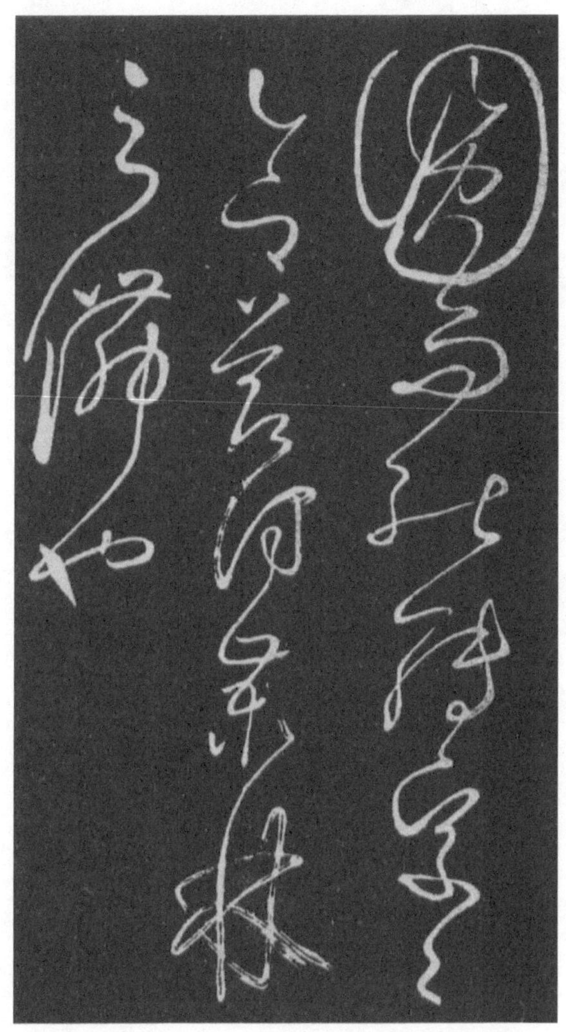

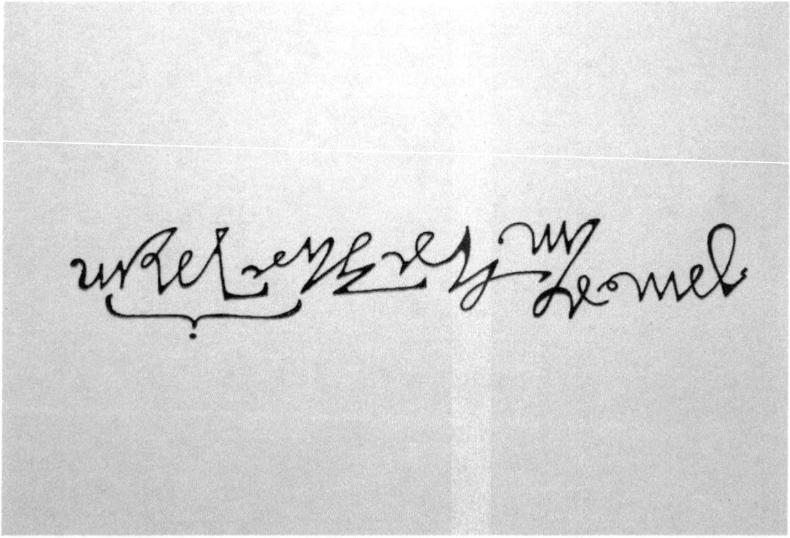

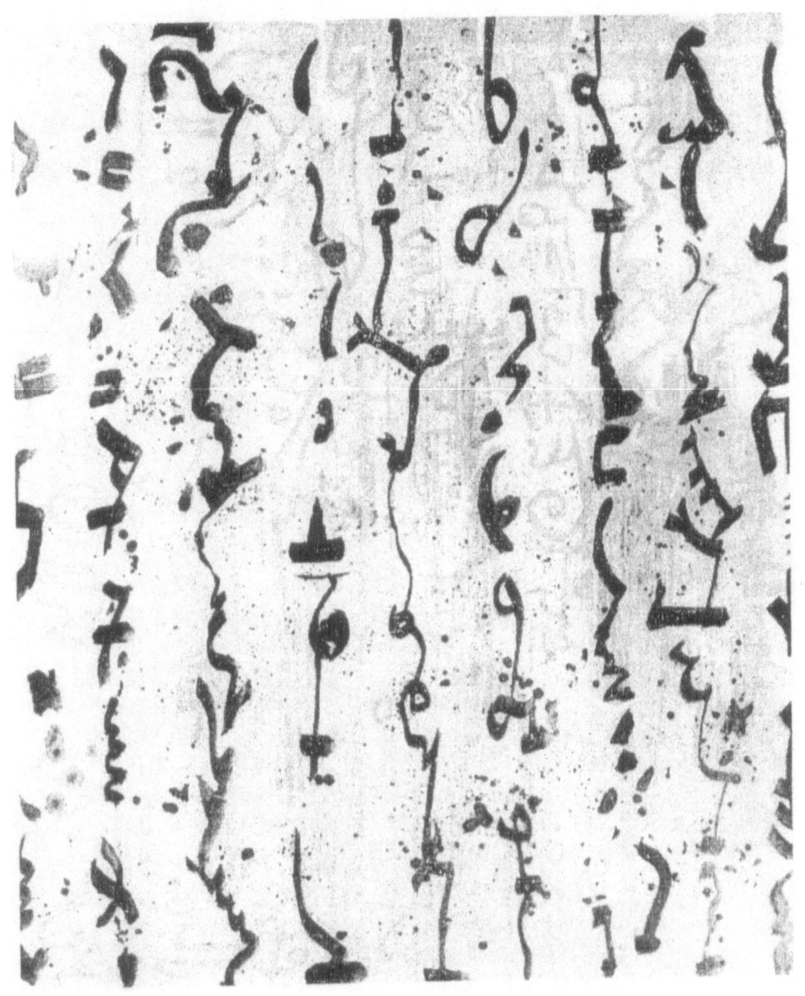

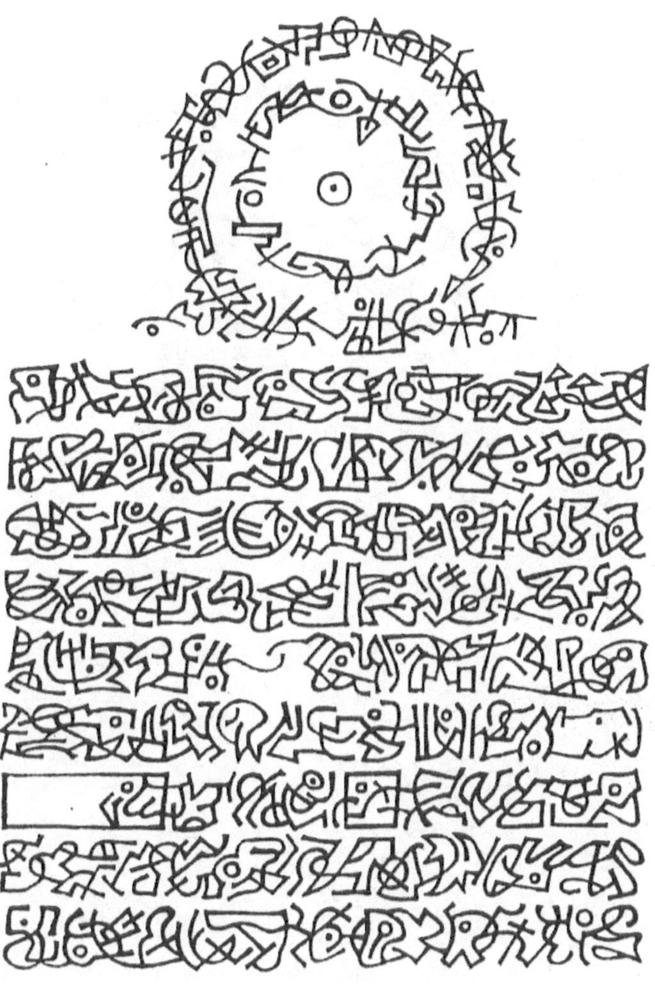

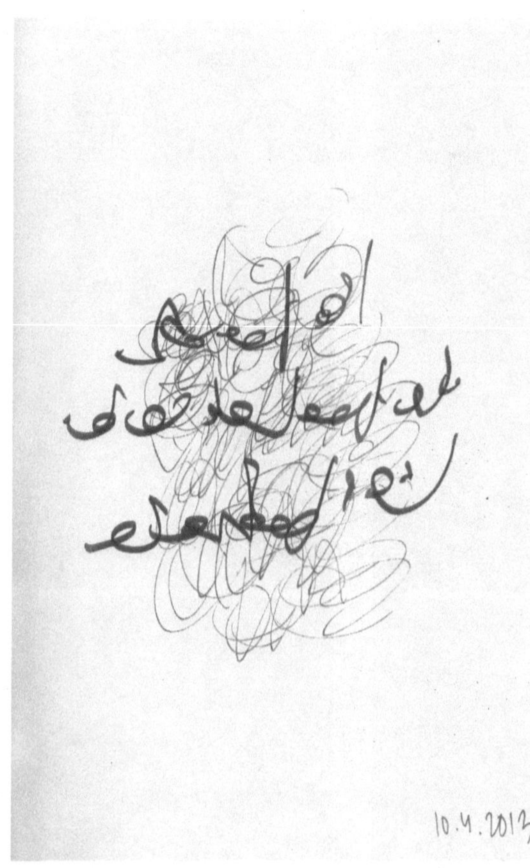
10.4.2013

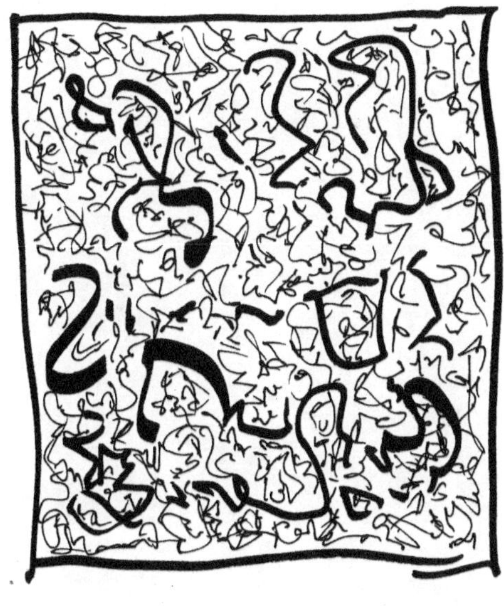

JpK 12/04.

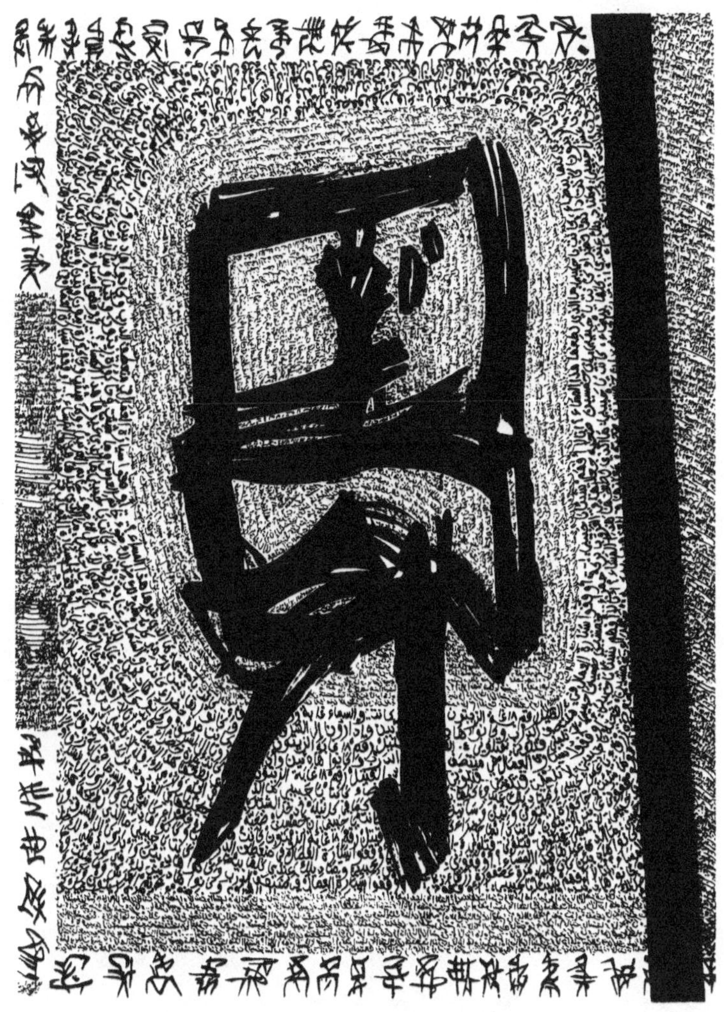

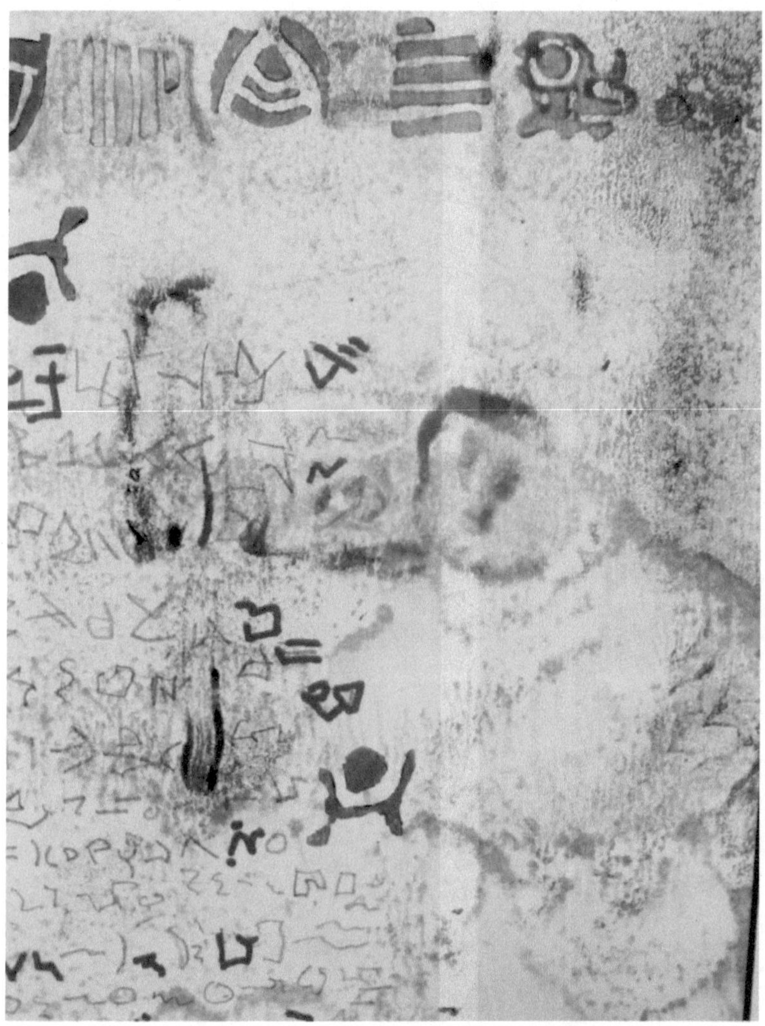

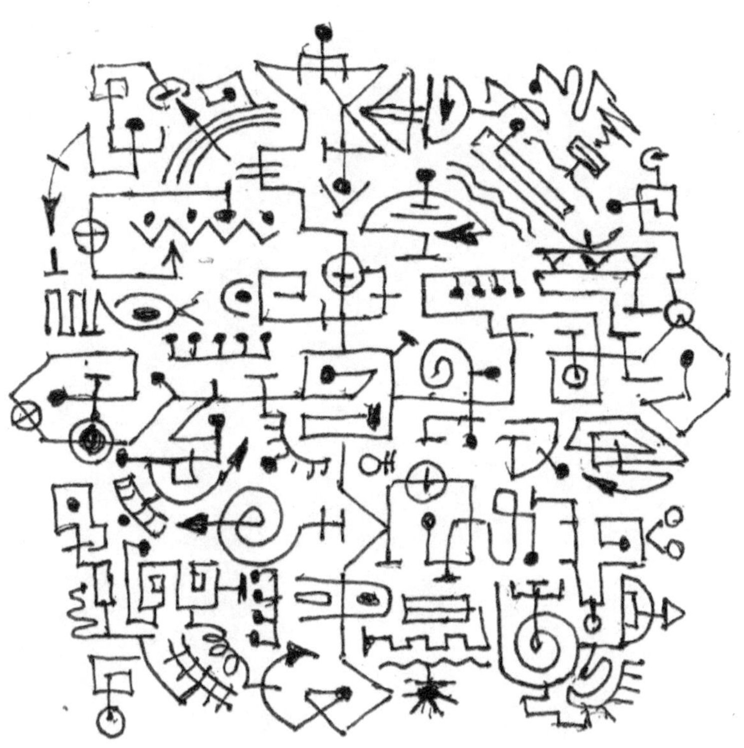

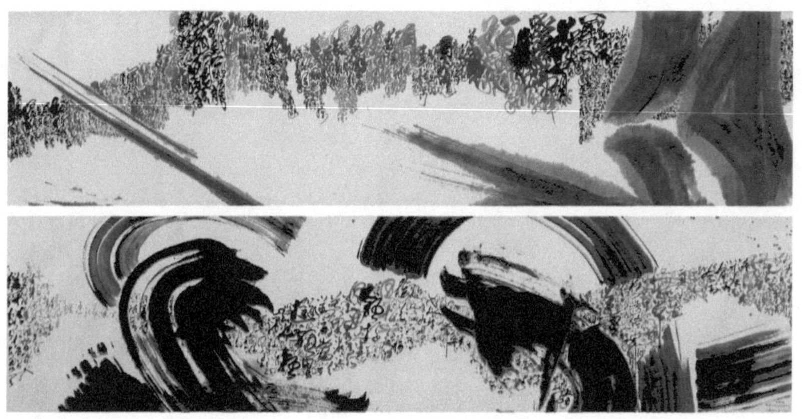

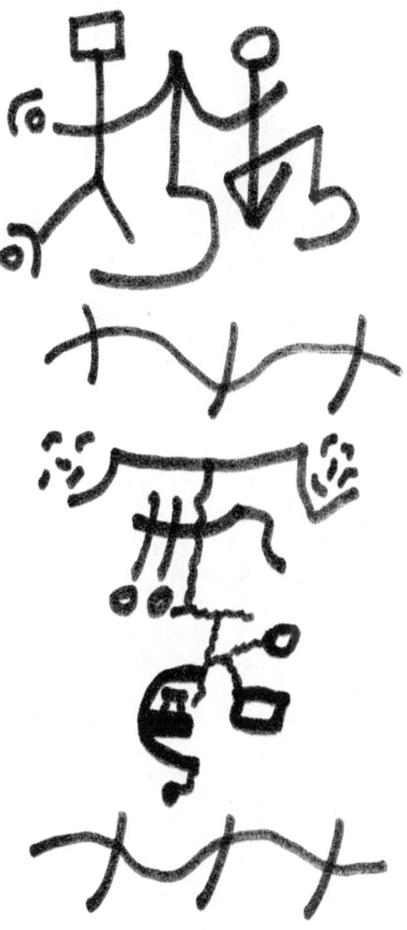

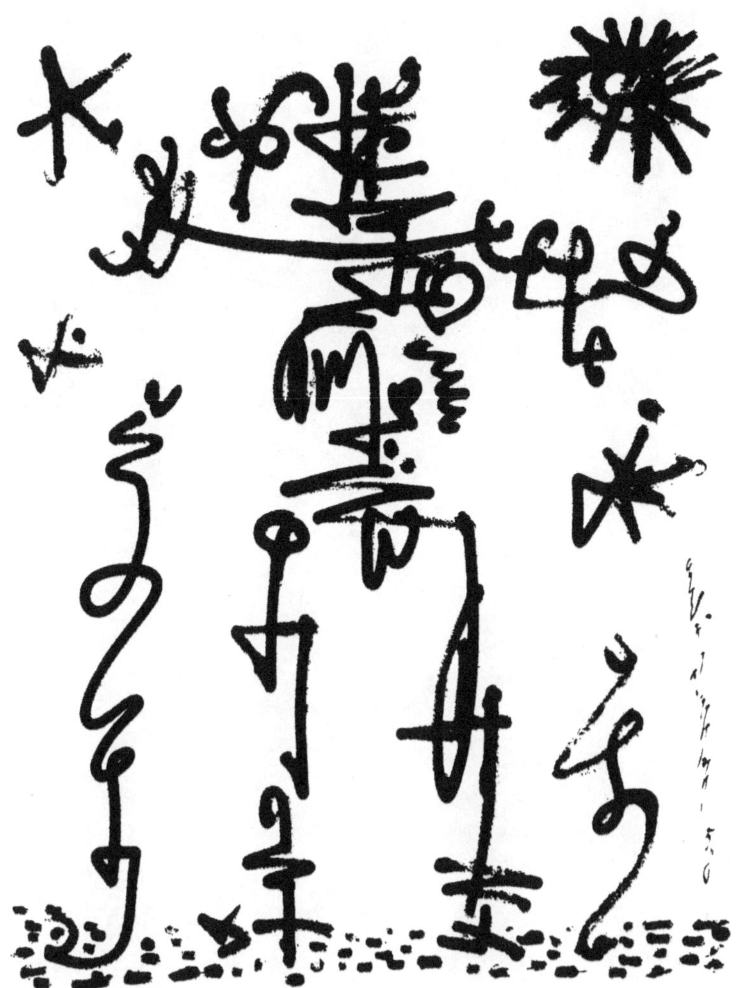

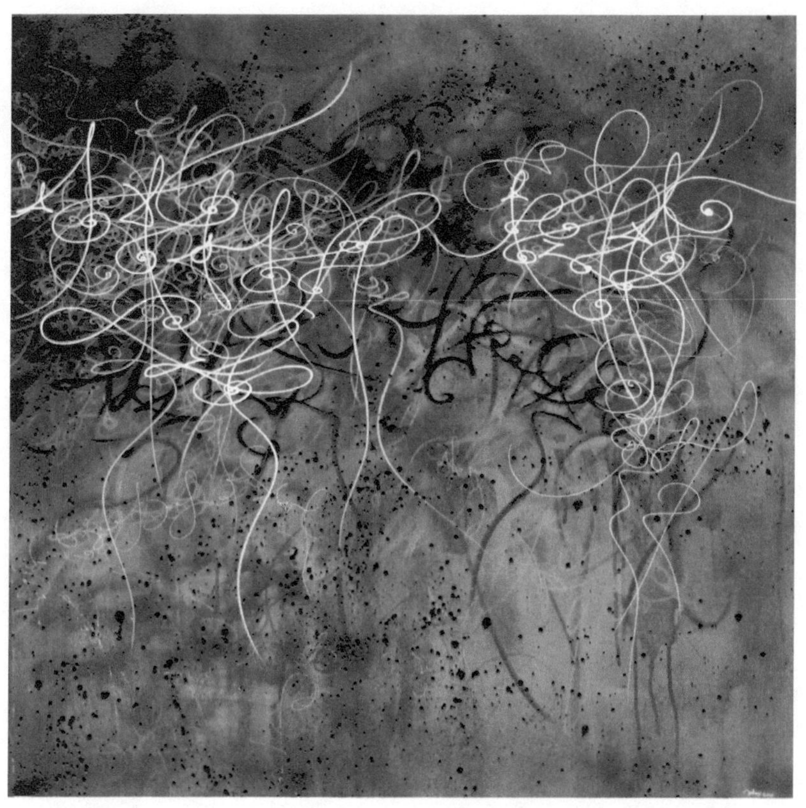

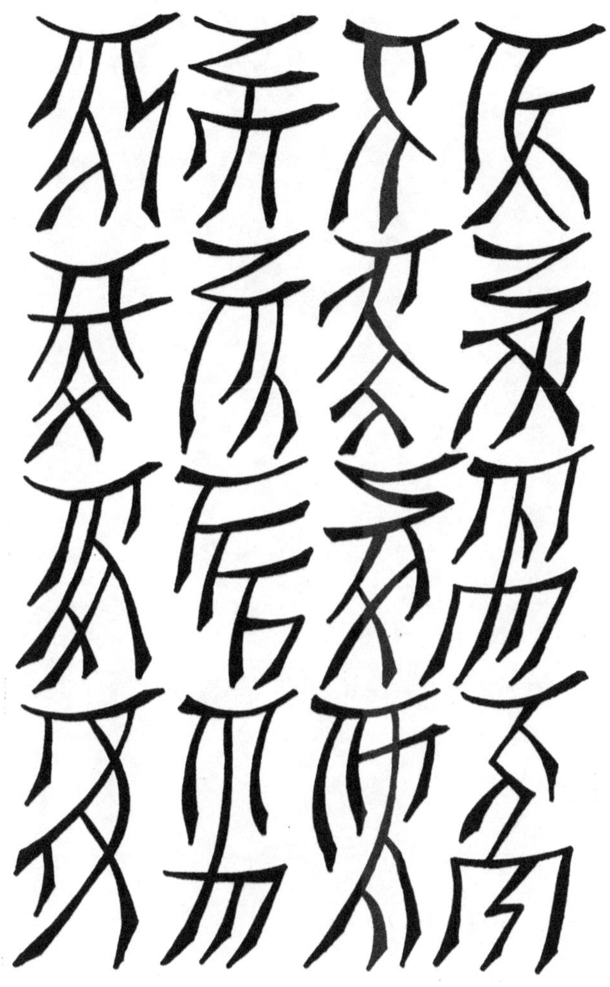

ALPHABET (2)

Henri Michaux
Octobre 27

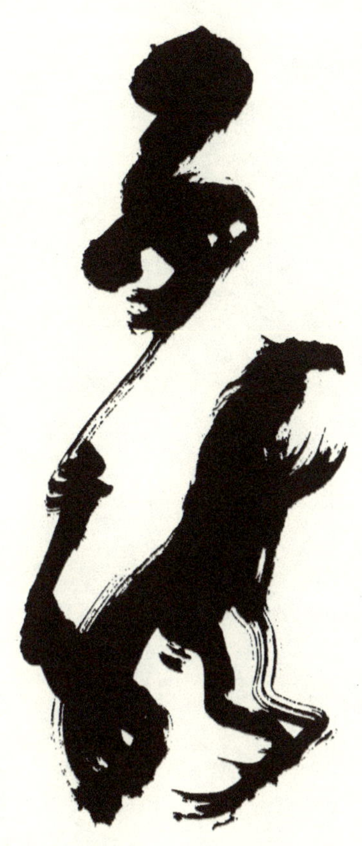

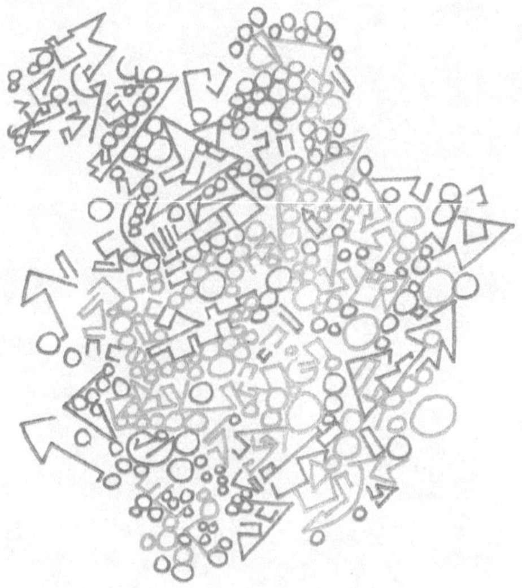

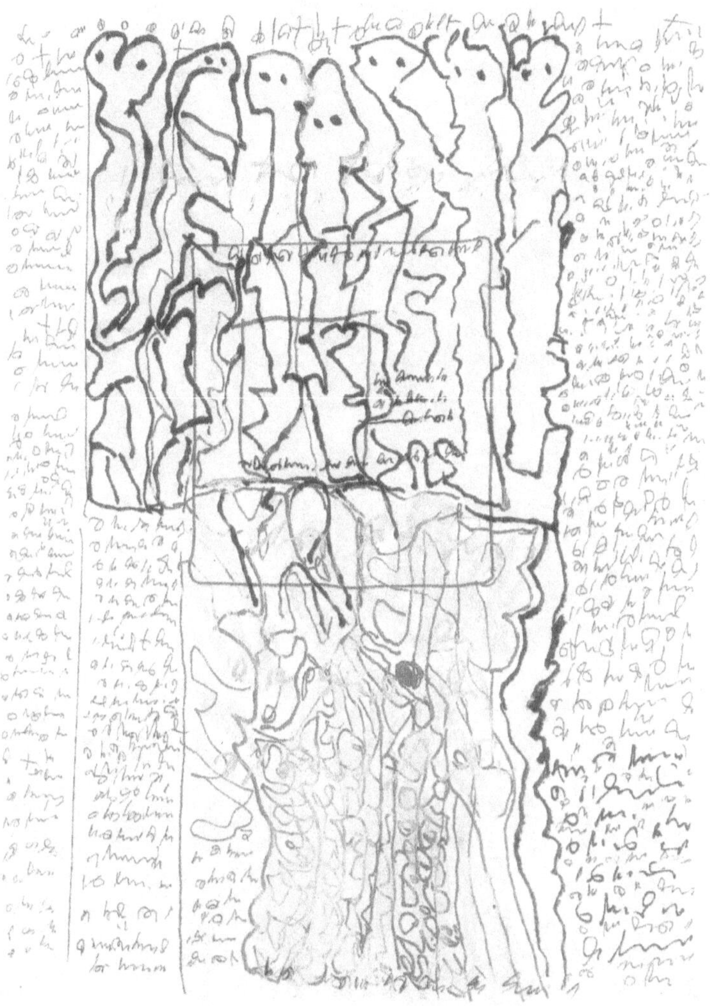

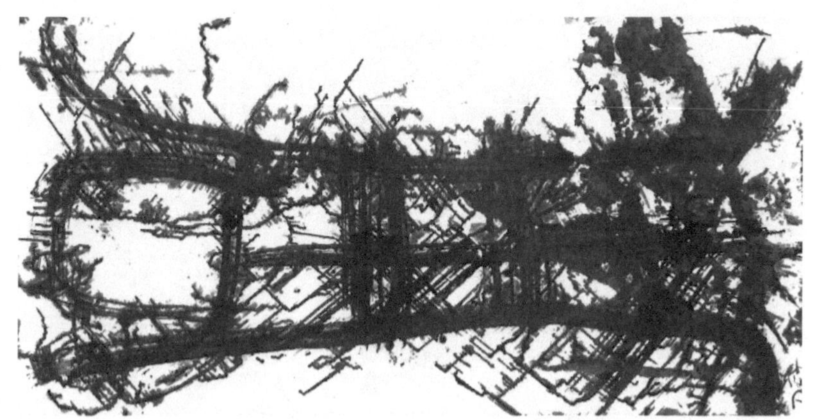

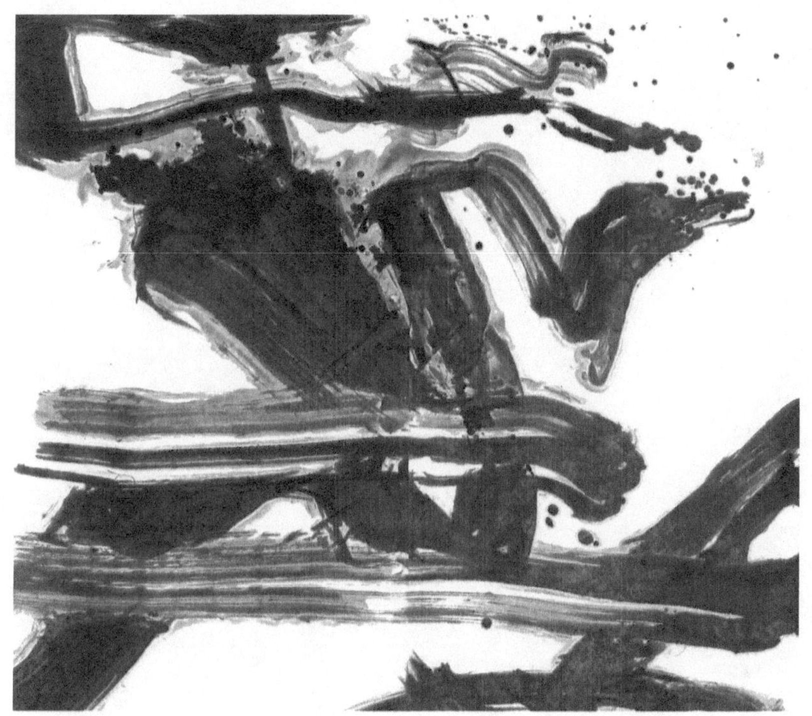

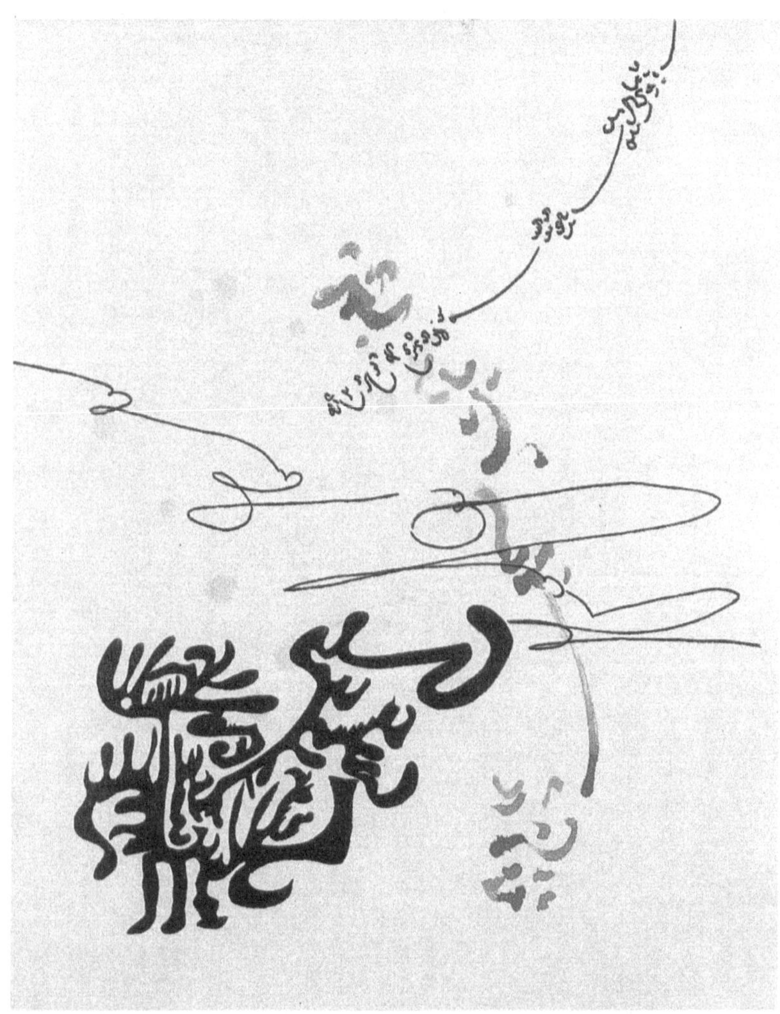

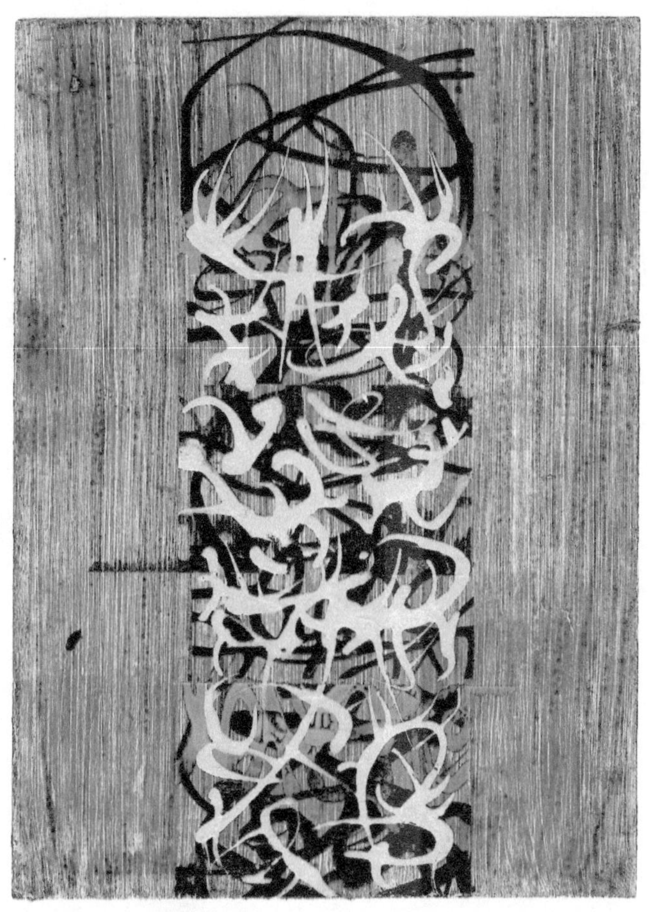

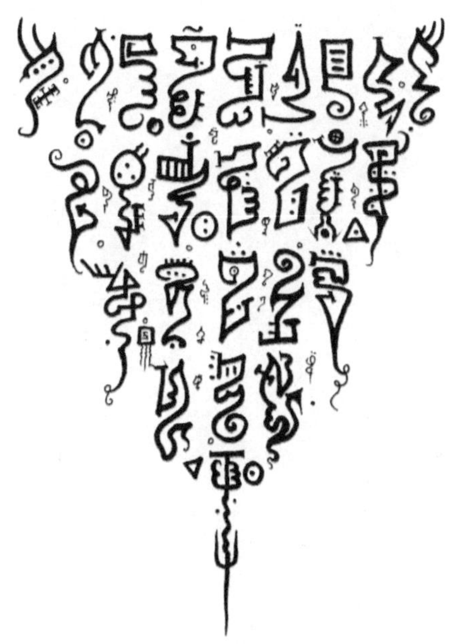

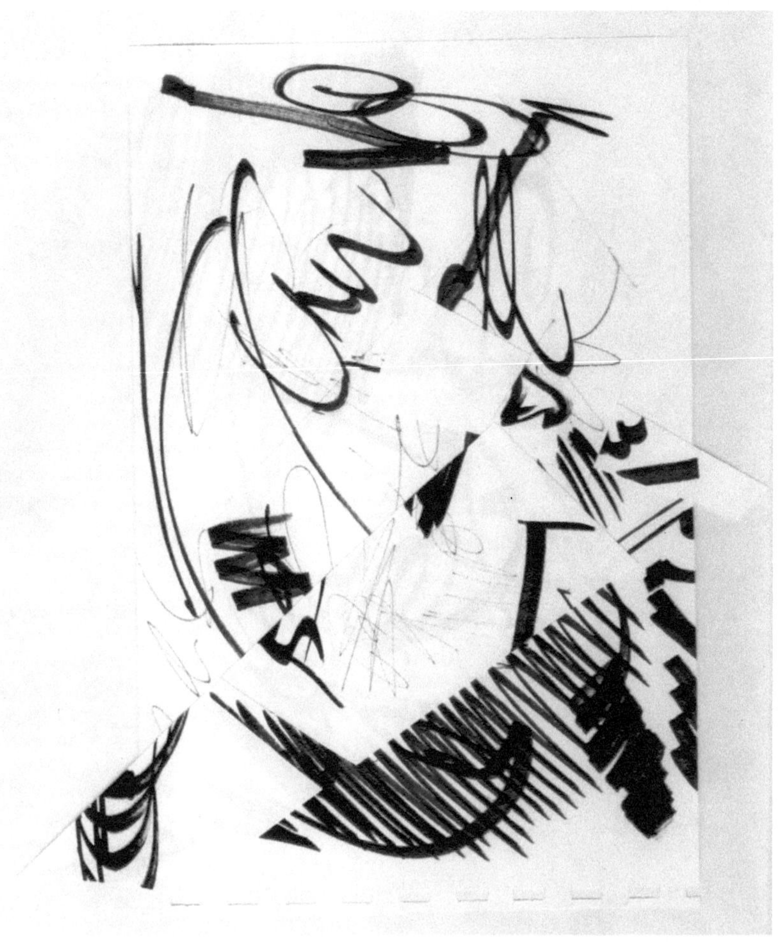

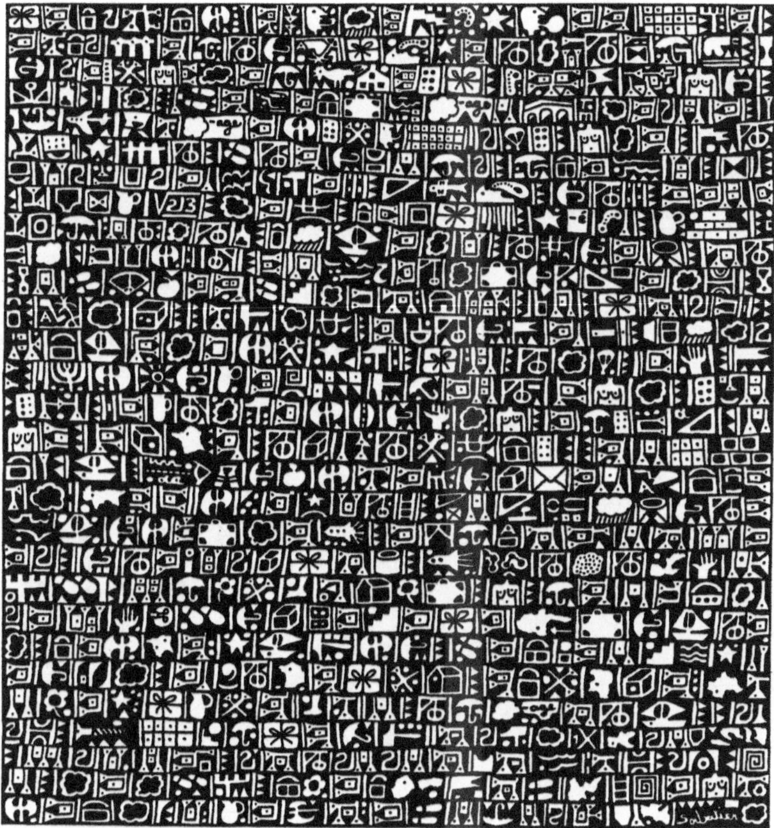
Sabatier

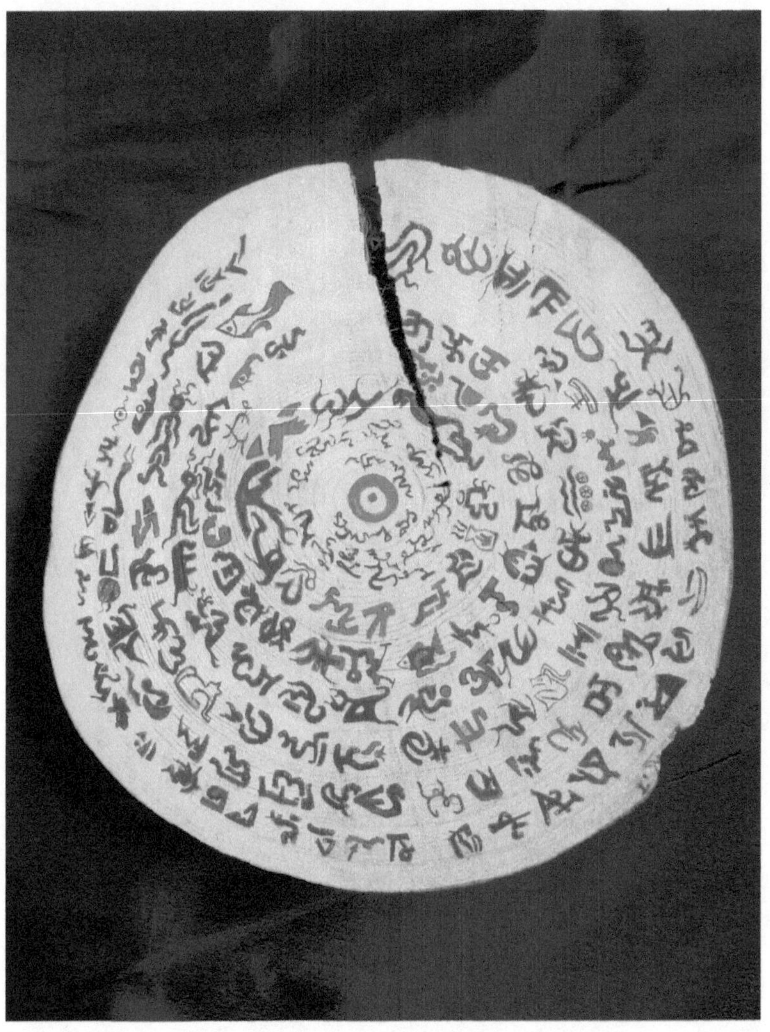

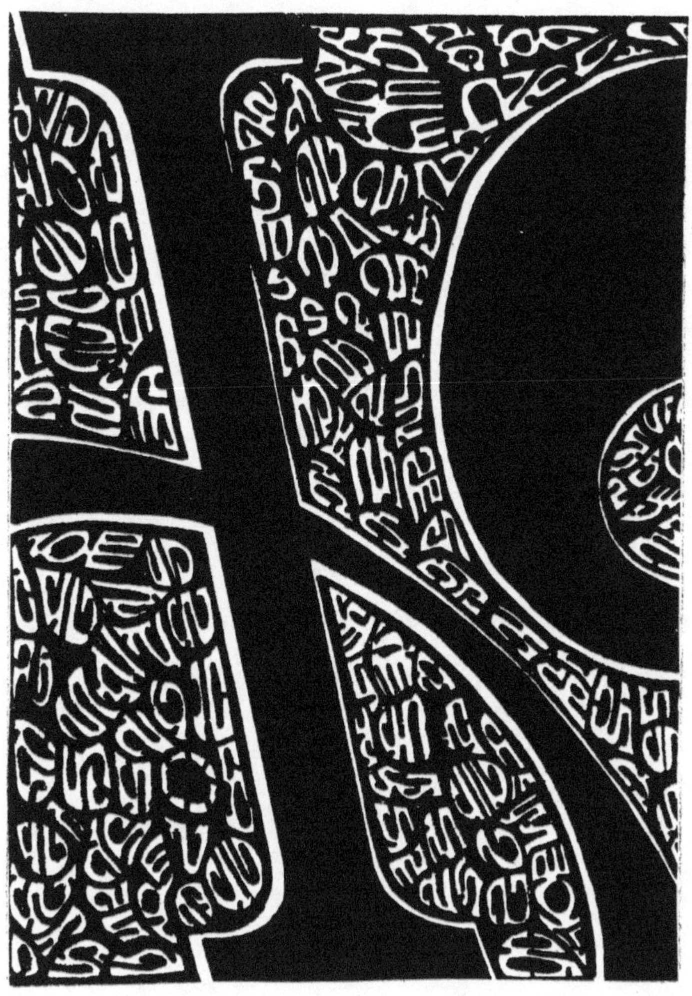

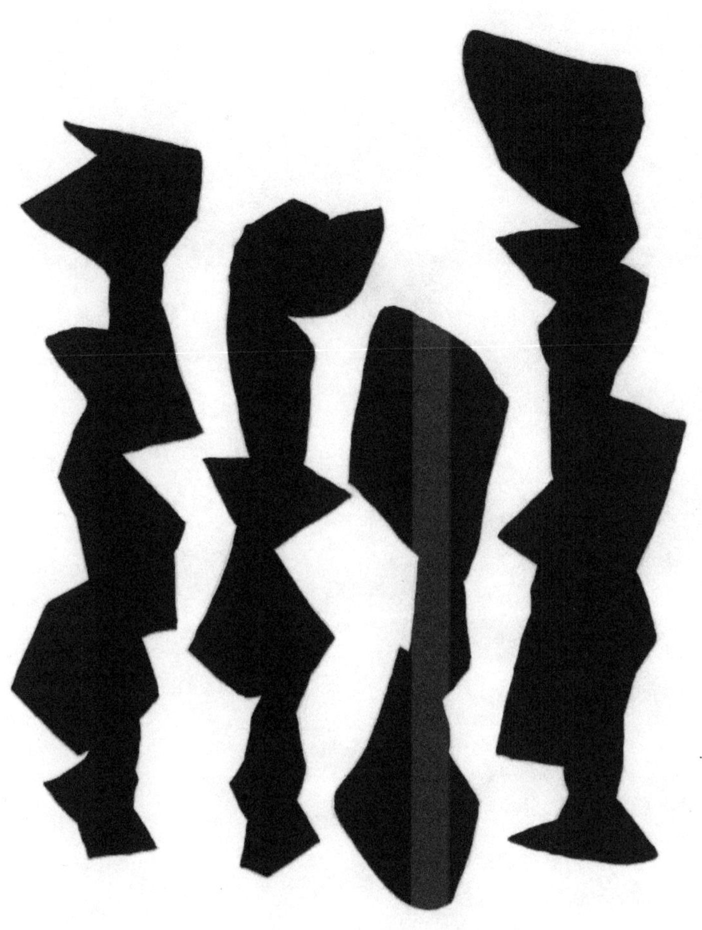

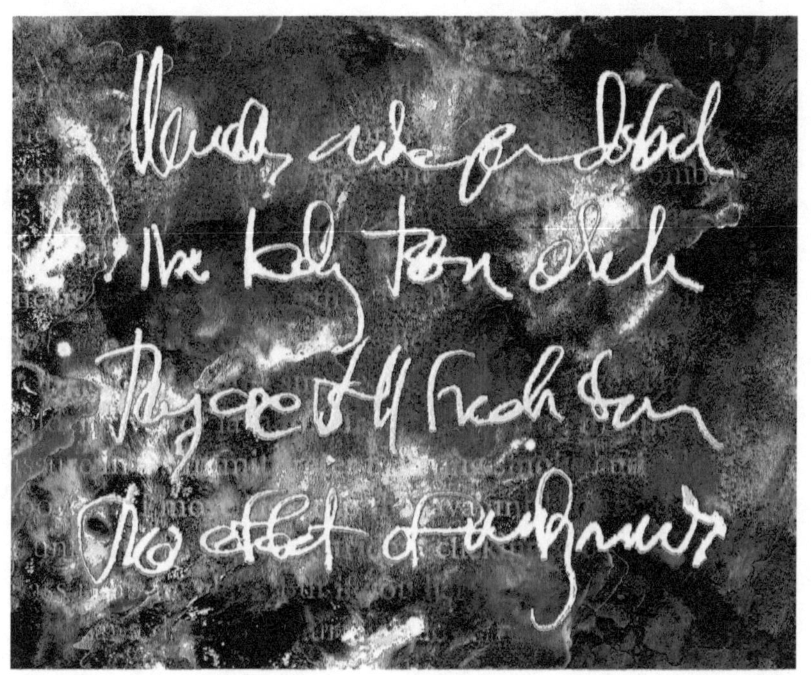

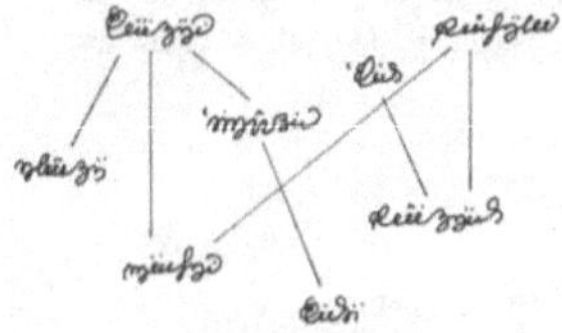

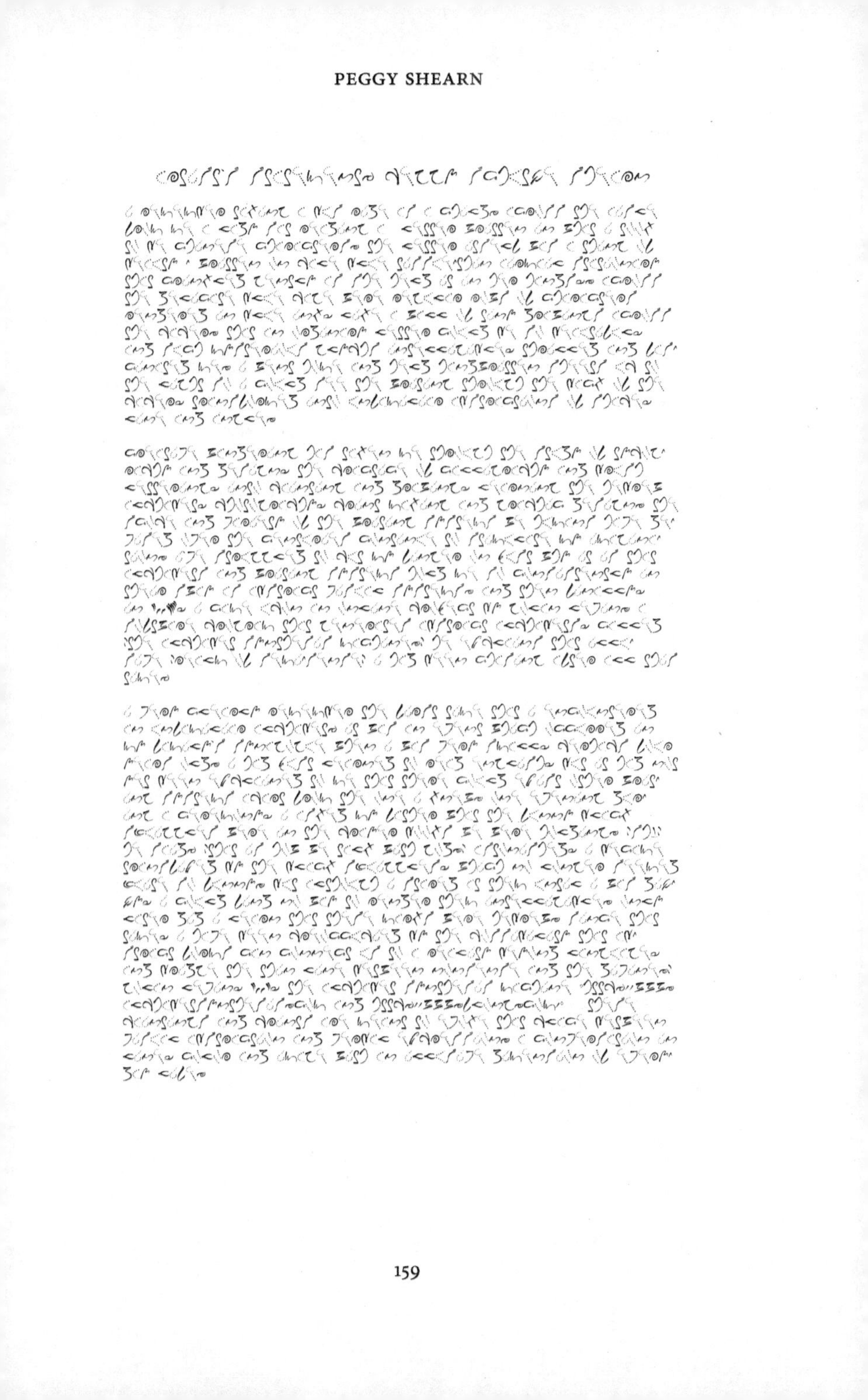

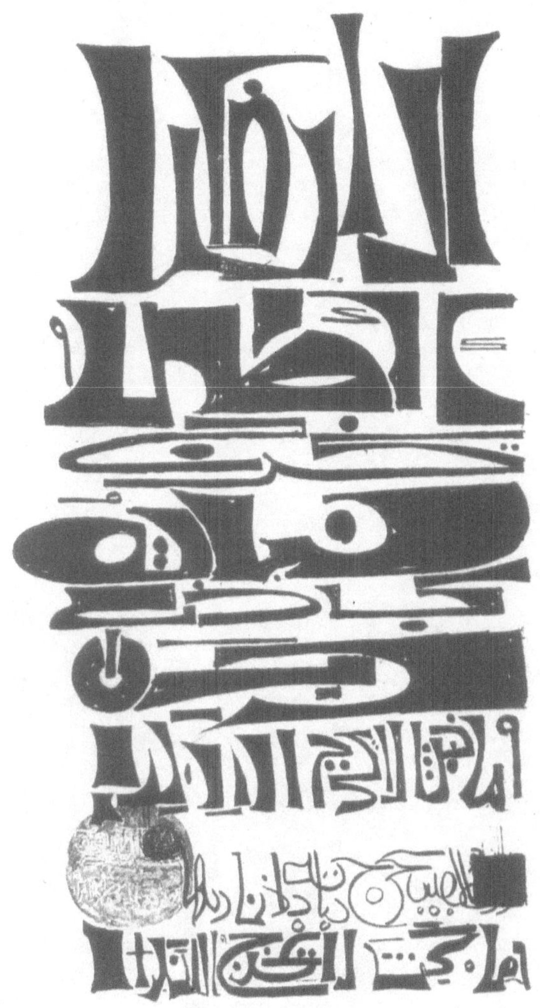

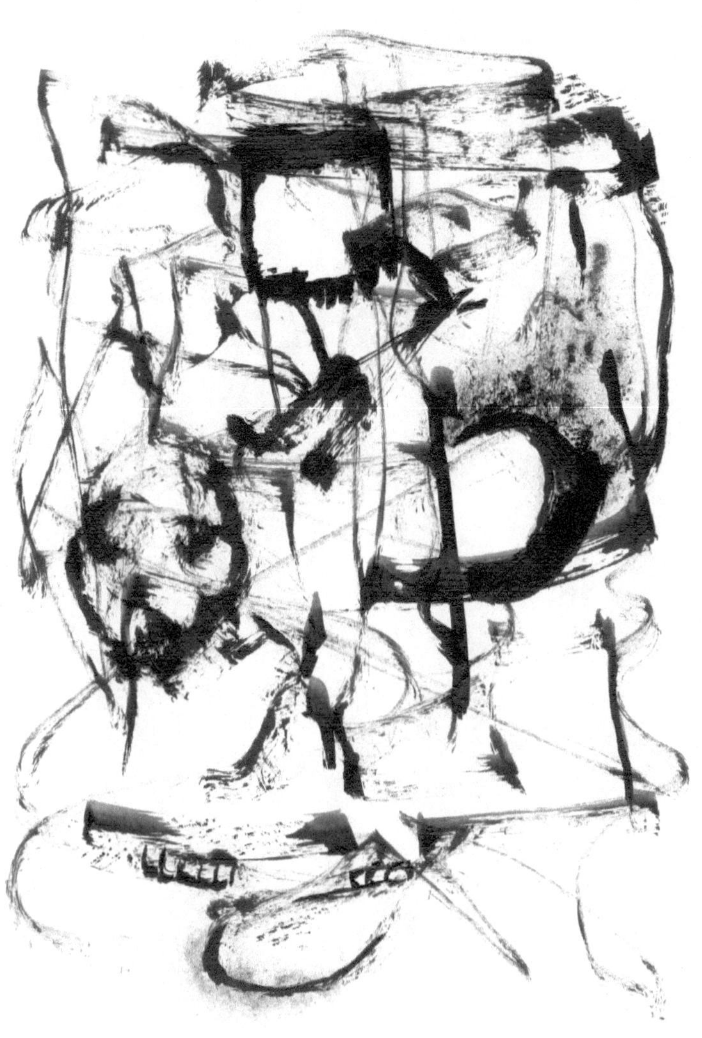

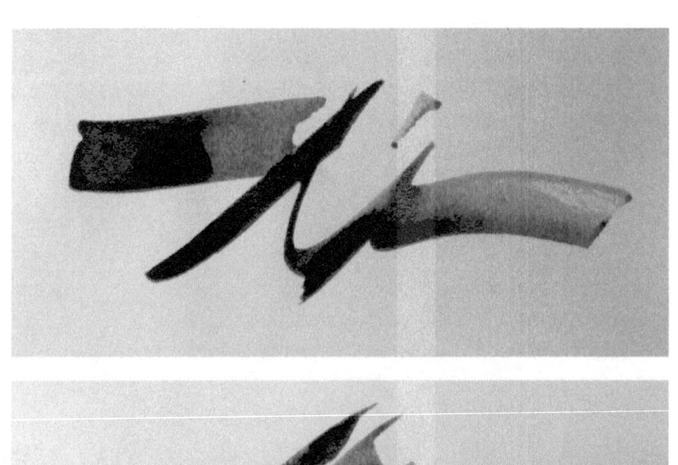

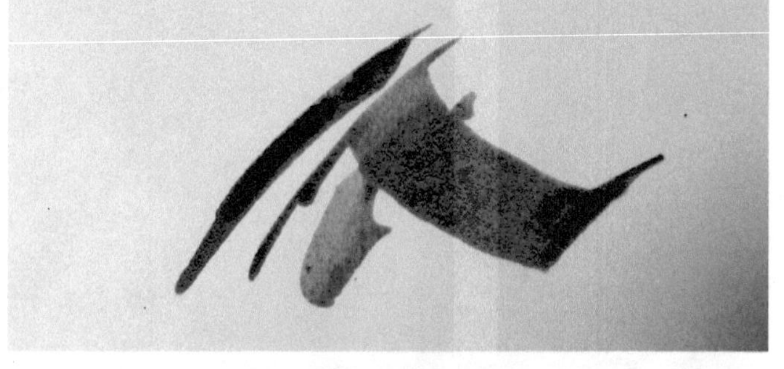

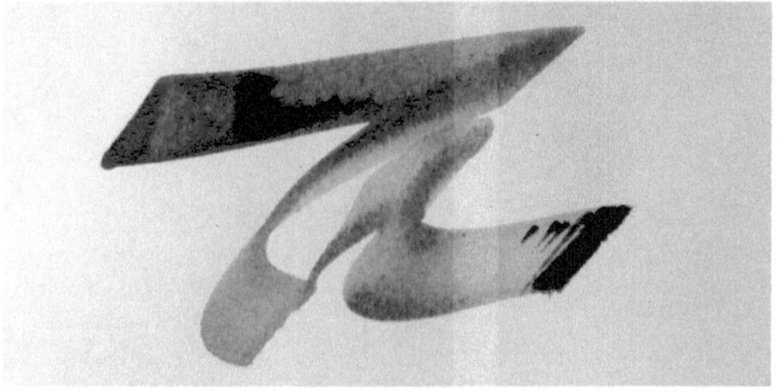

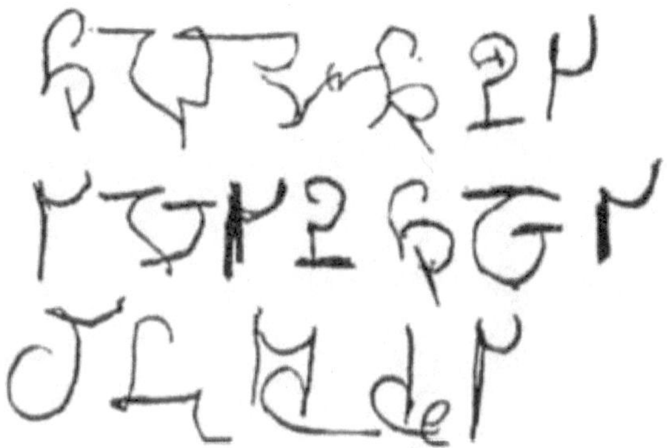

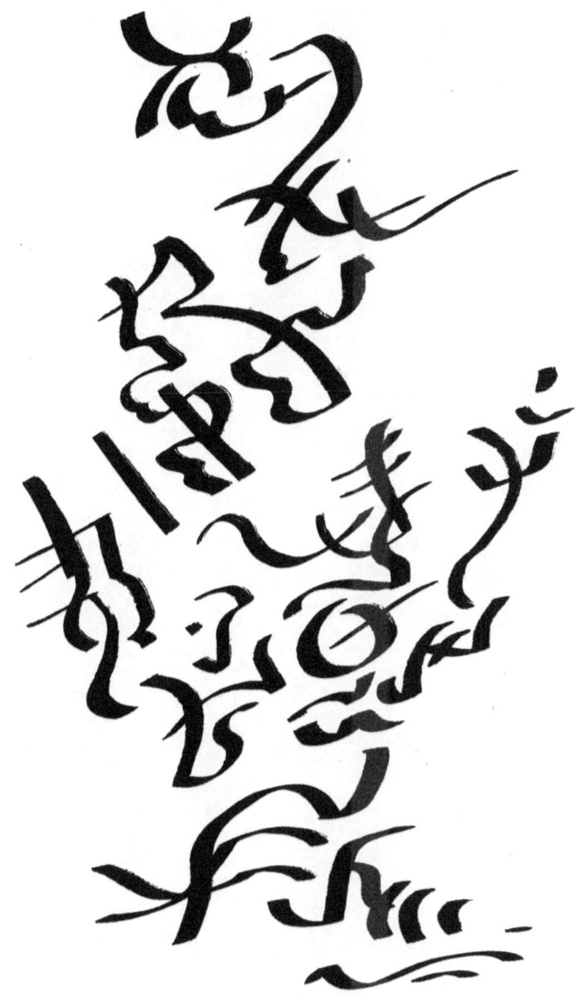

Dearest Love ——,

be that
that night we danced under the stars,
ered with me that our love felt
eventually turn us down, not
the nature of the mind nor the
depths of the heart.

Yours forever,
[illegible]

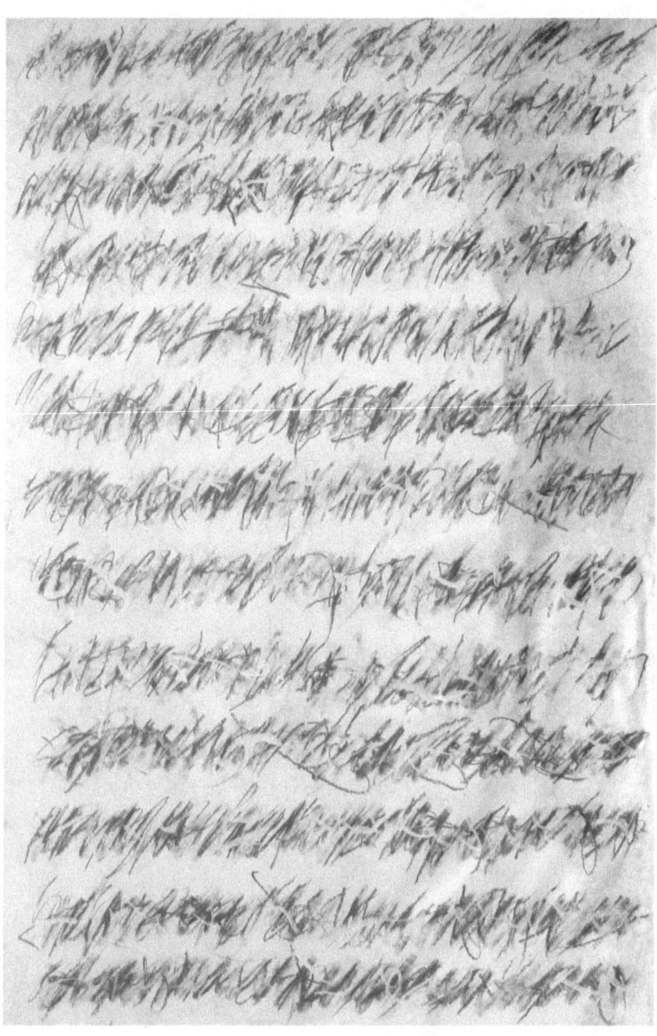

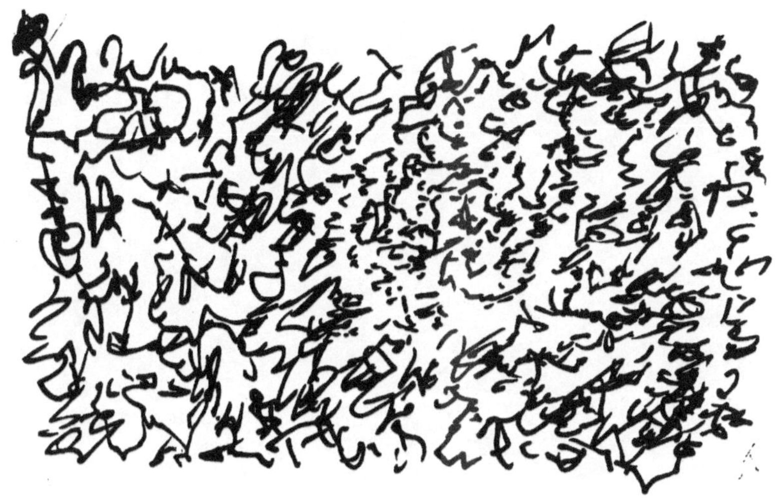

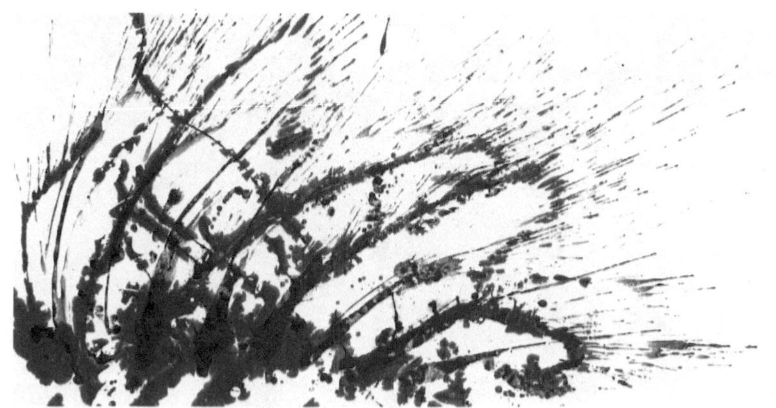

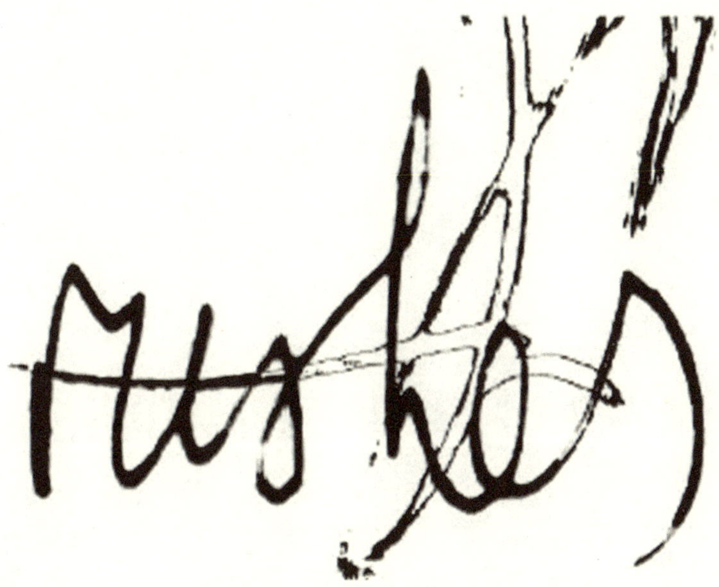

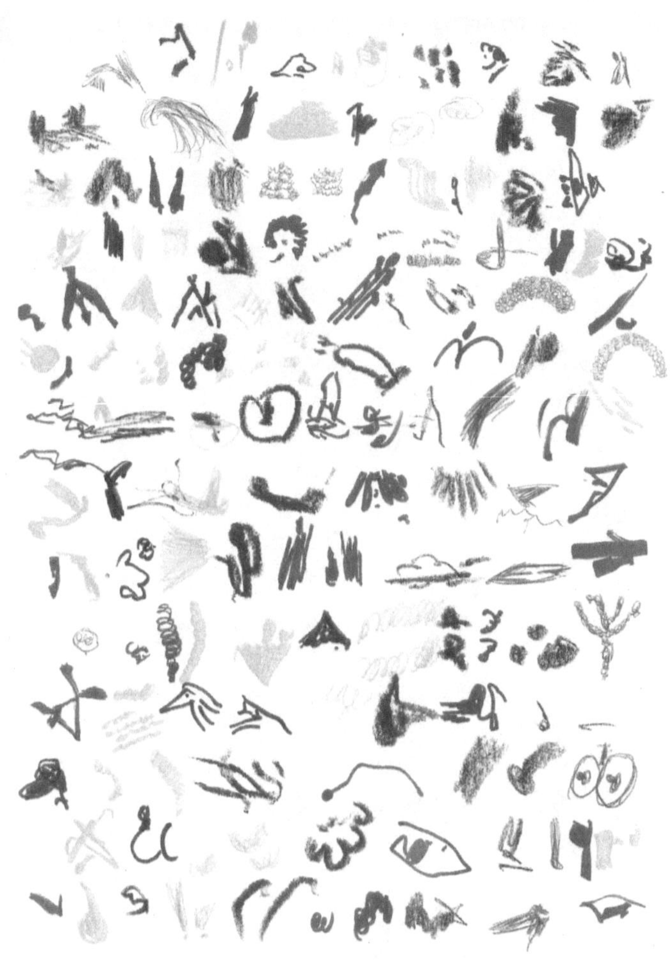

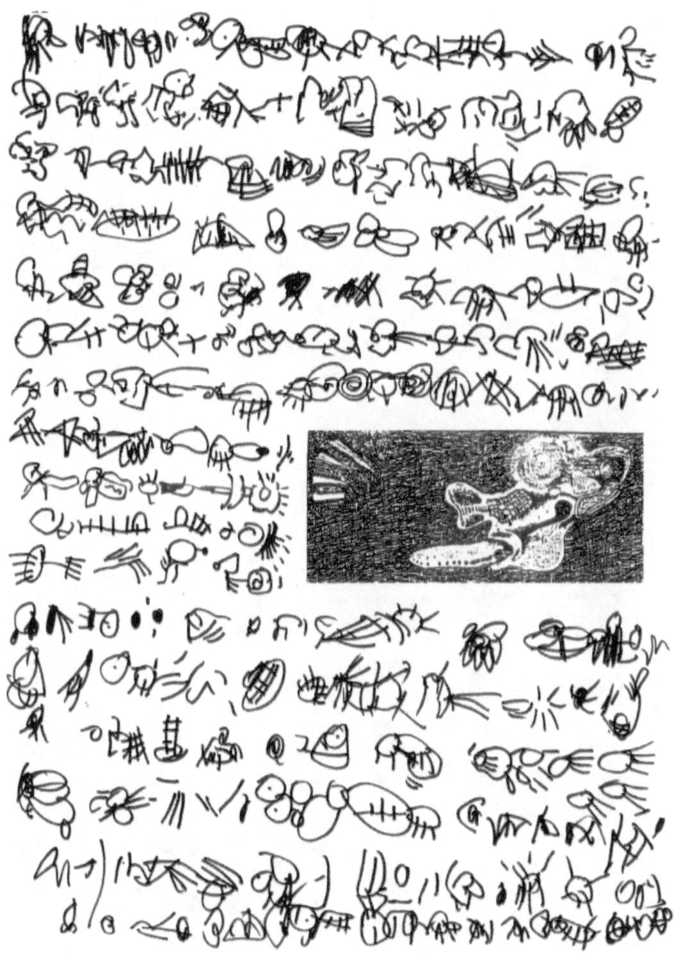

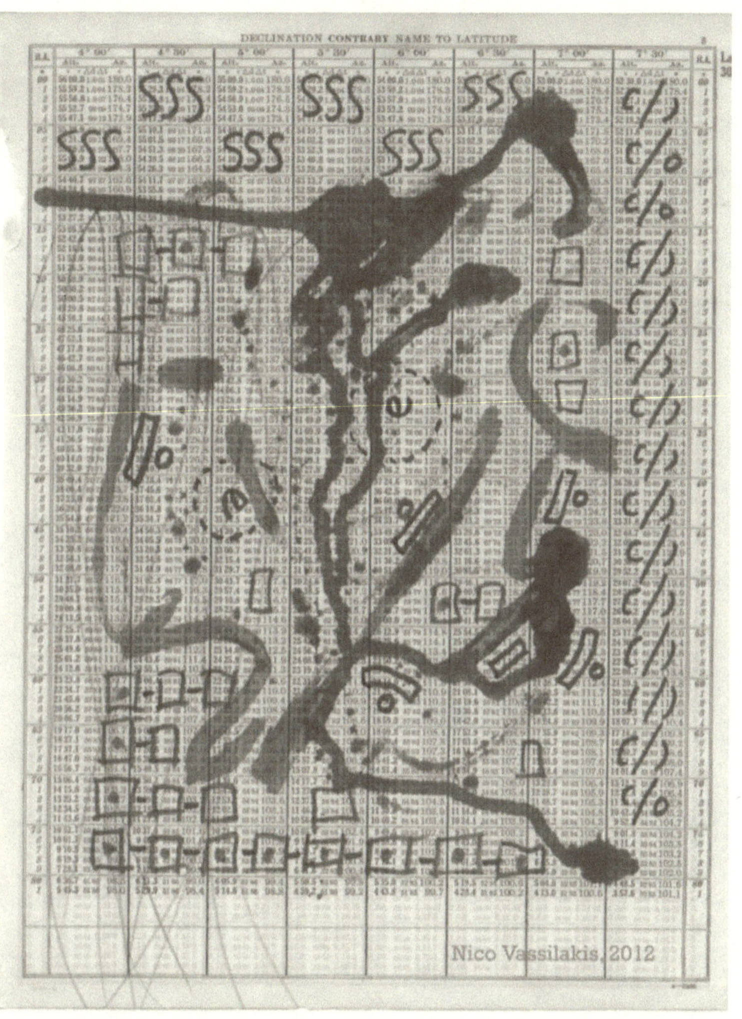
DECLINATION CONTRARY NAME TO LATITUDE
Nico Vassilakis, 2012

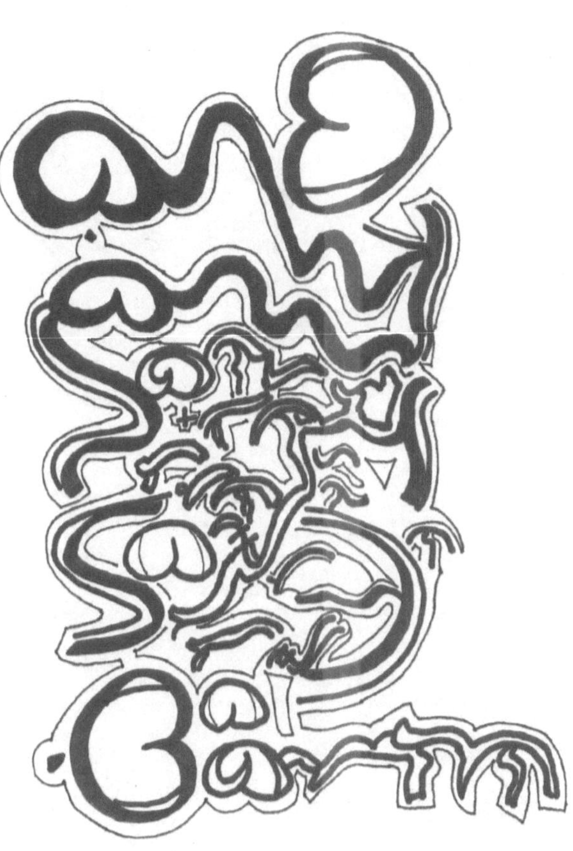

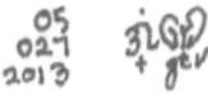

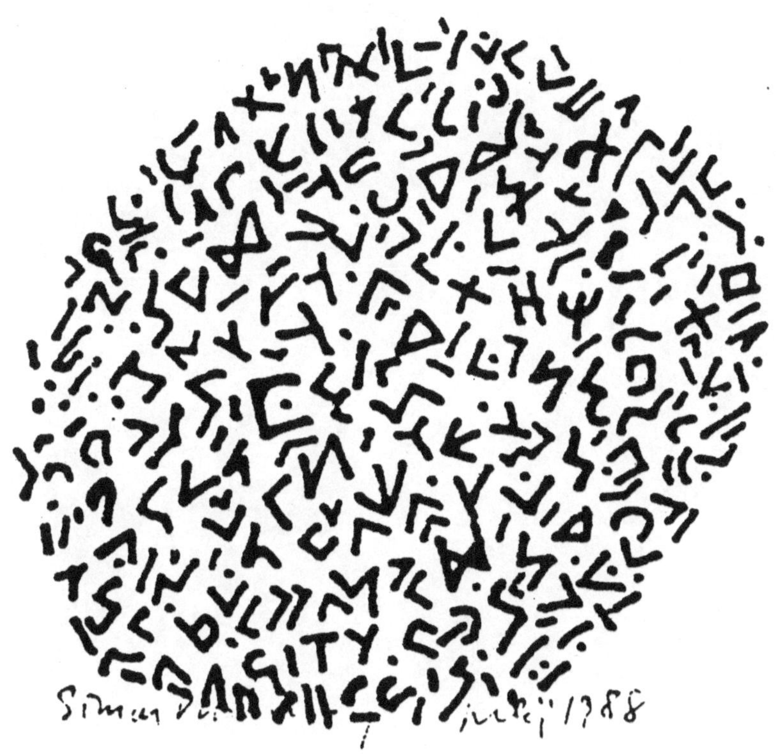

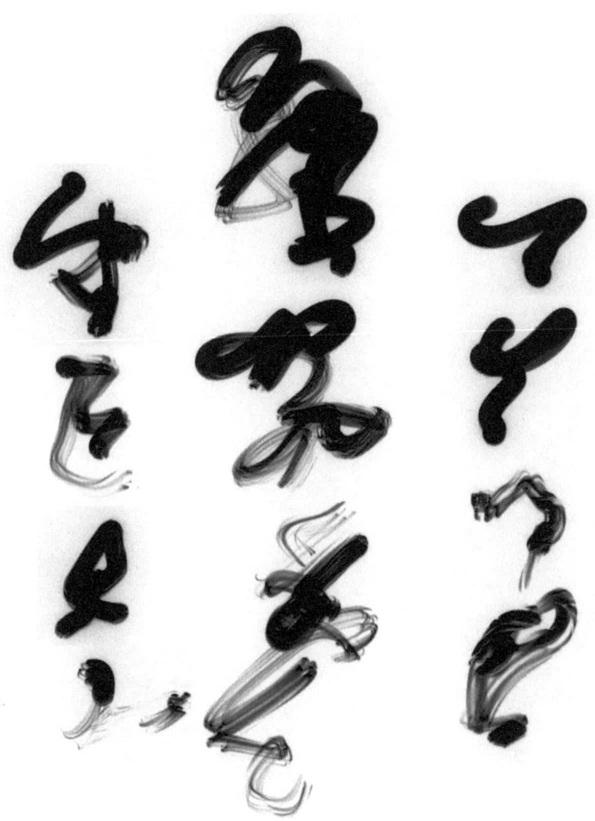

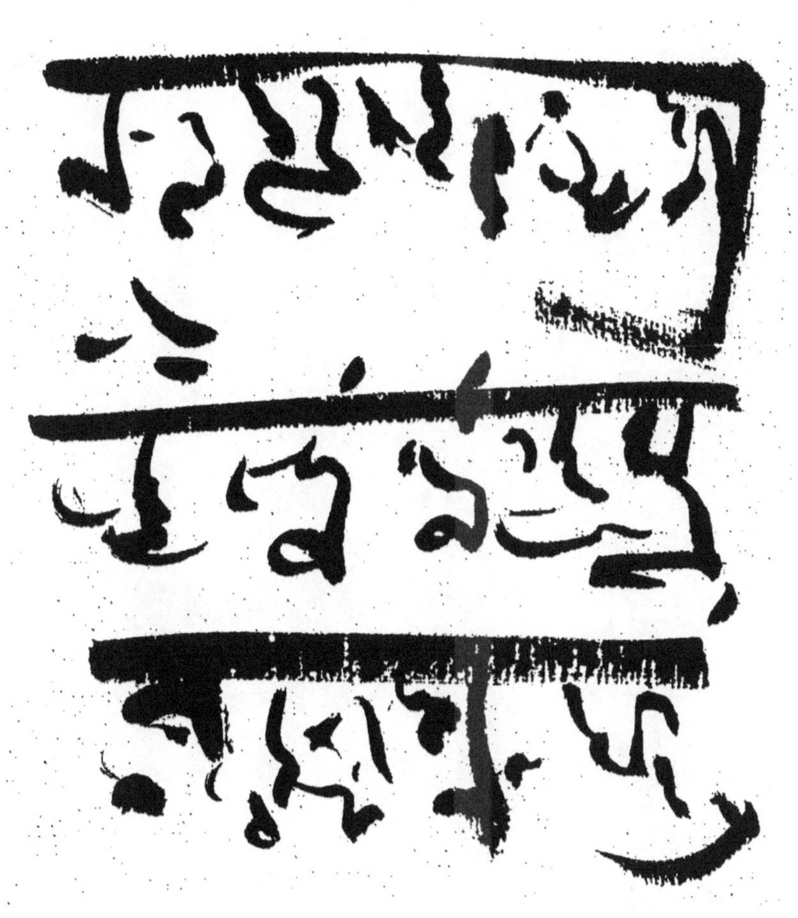

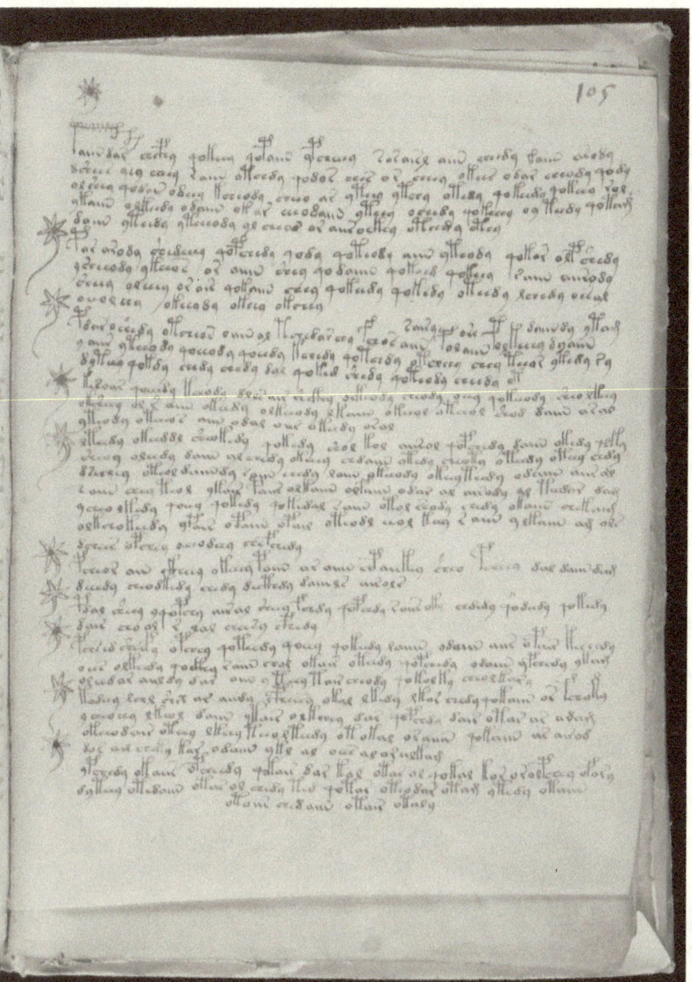
105

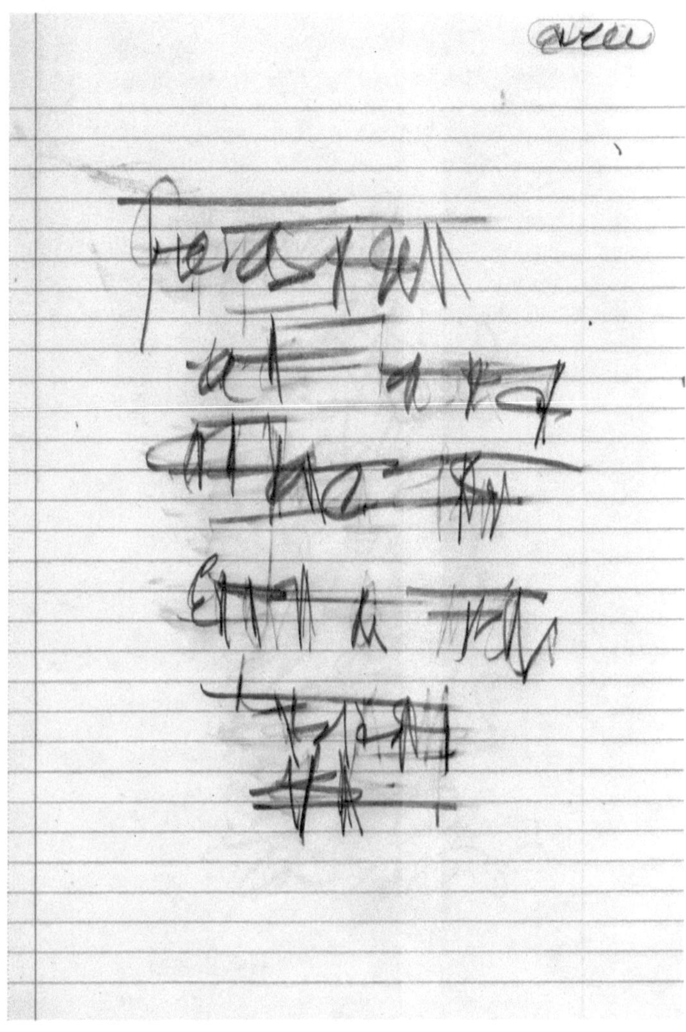

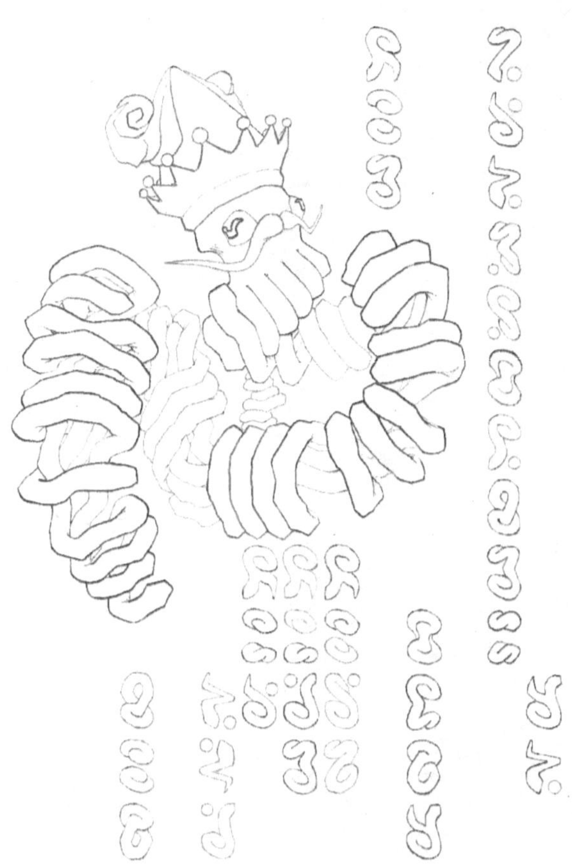

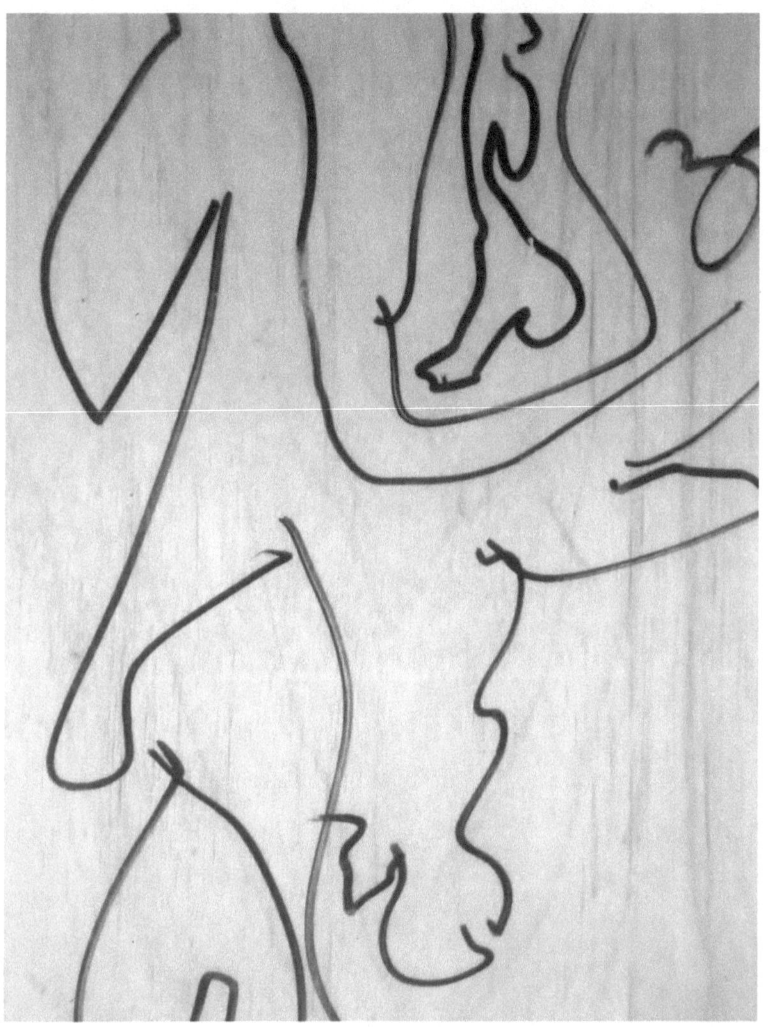

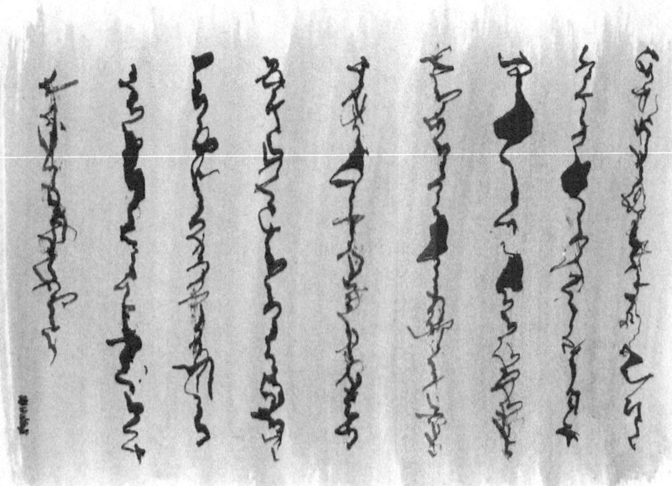

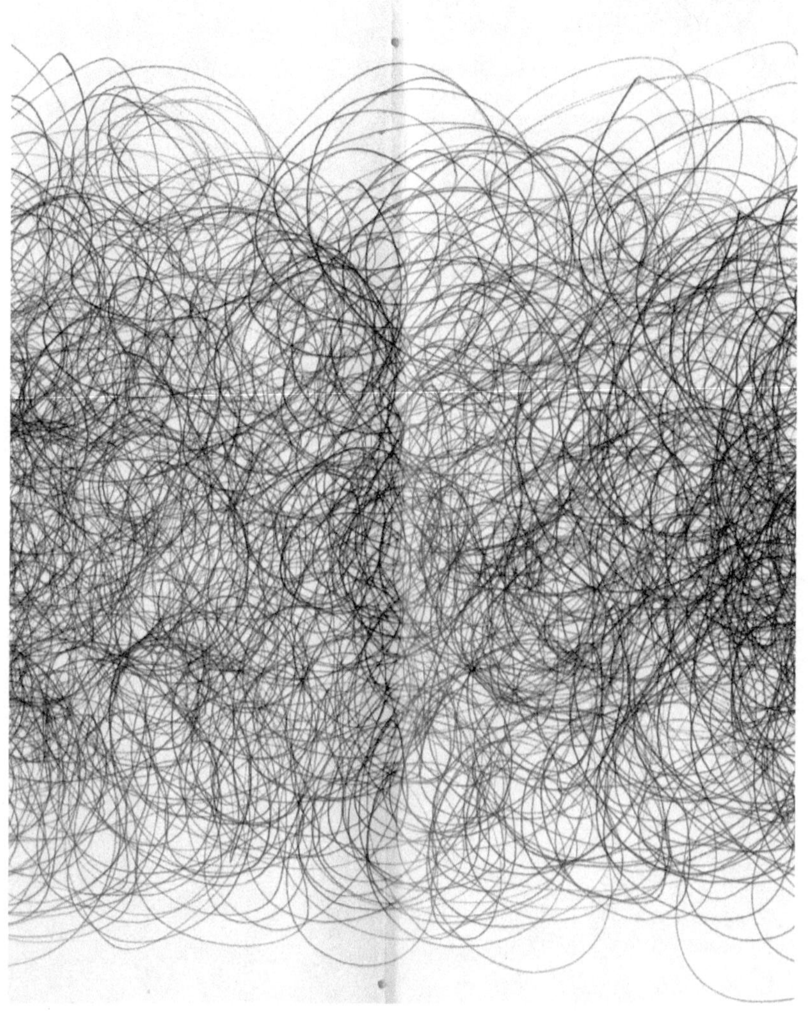

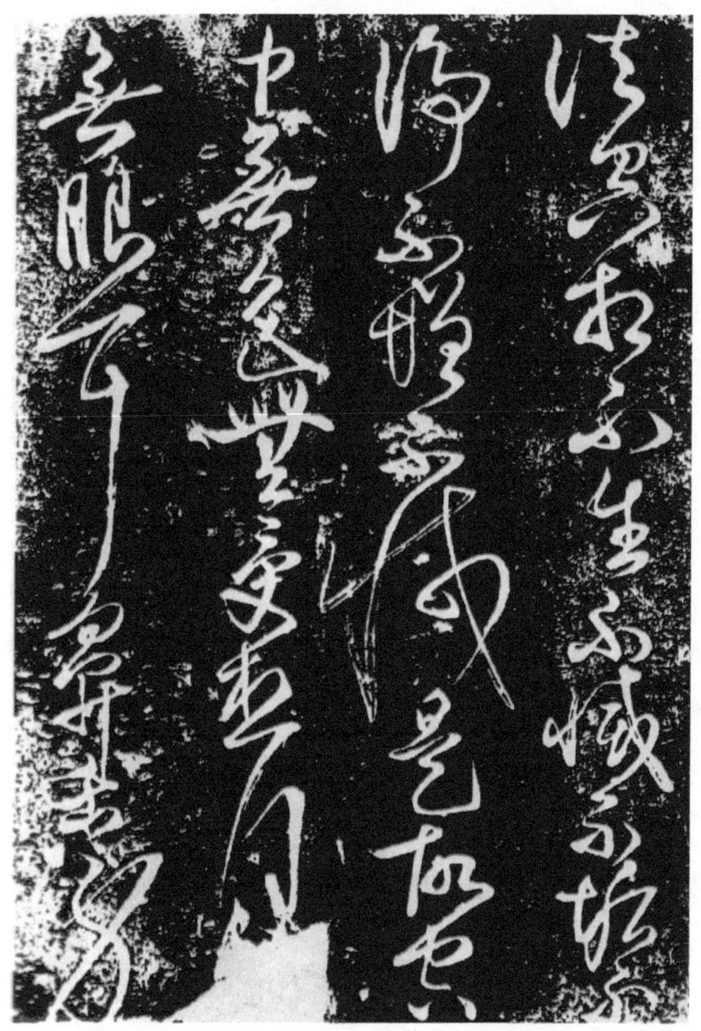

Acknowledgments

The editors would like to extend their gratitude to the following people: Françoise Favretto, Christian Yde Frostholm, Theo Green, John & Dorothy Jacobson, Suzanne Lecht, Thomas Bidstrup Jeppesen, Vũ Thùy Trang, and everyone who contributed to *Asemic* magazine and *The New Post-Literate* blog.

www.ingramcontent.com/pod-product-compliance
Lightning Source LLC
LaVergne TN
LVHW091140080826
845145LV00008B/2214

* 9 7 8 9 0 8 1 7 0 9 1 7 0 *